# CONVERSATIONS THAT CHANGE US

# CONVERSATIONS THAT CHANGE US

### Learning the Arts of Theological Reflection Second Edition

## Joyce E. Bellous and Dan Sheffield

Tall Pine Press

Edmonton, AB

Conversations That Change Us- Second Edition

Copyright © 2017 Joyce E. Bellous

Published 2017 by Tall Pine Press

Edmonton, Alberta, Canada

www.tallpinepress.com

Cover Design by Lisa Howden

Illustrations by Dan Sheffield, Joyce E. Bellous and Lisa Howden

A cataloguing record for this publication is available from Library and Archives Canada.

ISBN: 978-0-9810149-4-4 (paperback)

# CONTENTS

# PREFACE

This book is an invitation. Read its theory and carry out its exercises and enjoy effective and fulfilling change in your life of faith. Record your process. Write out your initial thoughts. Observe what happens to those thoughts. Keep notes on your insights.

The book has three parts. Part One includes three models and one practice, *Lectio Divina*, that provide clear and accessible approaches to conversing with God, other people and ourselves. We hope you engage with these methods and put them to use as you begin to work through the book. We also introduce the notion of theological reflection as a conversation with God, within yourselves and with the Christian community. It's a conversation in which we encounter the humanizing gaze of the Living God breaking into our alienation and our conflicts. As we begin to really dialogue, we stop and listen to our thoughts, observe our actions and give attention to our assumptions.

As we engage in these ways, we allow other people to witness the story we tell ourselves about God, our own lives and the meaning we give to being human. That story is a personal narrative each one of us has been gathering and telling since we were very young. It continues to shape and inform how we understand other people, world, the God and ourselves.

The second part of the book focuses on personal theological reflection. There are practices that help teach the arts of theological reflection and form a foundation on which Christians think about and express the faith they profess to hold. The purpose of these practices and perspectives is to expand our vision and rethink the ways we've always seen the world. There are exercises and case studies that help formulate the origins and trajectory of your own Christian views. There is a perspective provided that helps identify whether your dominant approach to faith is based in a heart, a head, an image or an action-based approach.

In working through the second part, it's essential to discover more about your faith style to see that other people may not share your way to being Christian, even though they too are followers of Jesus. Just as our encounter with God can't easily be placed in merely human categories—God is other—so our engagement with other believers must allow for differences to emerge and flourish.[1]

The second part includes an adaptation of *Lectio Divina* that allows you to consider your reading of scripture in light of your personal history and experience. In working through the practice, you learn to give yourself your own true and best reasons for the way you tend to read the Bible and practice the Christian faith. In general, theological reflection is an educational exercise. The theories in parts one and two identify principles and presents methods for structuring and understanding how you carry out personal theological reflection when on your own or when you're with other people that you minister among or lead.

The third part of *Conversations* differs from the first two primarily because it's focused on collaborative theological reflection. Collaborative theological reflection is demonstrated through a case study that is divided into three exercises.

Early Christians reflected theologically together and turned the world upside down. This book invites you to ask what you long to accomplish as you minister in God's Kingdom and in Jesus' name. We hope that reading the book and working through its exercises will help you realize Kingdom goals in your ministry. The arts of theological reflection, when done well, bring powerful results in forming Christian community.

*The Authors*

**Dr. Joyce Bellous** is Professor of Christian Faith Education at Taylor Seminary in Edmonton, Alberta. She taught previously for 16 years at McMaster Divinity College in Hamilton, Ontario.

**Rev. Dan Sheffield** served for many years as Director of Global and Intercultural Ministries for The Free Methodist Church in Canada. He is an adjunct lecturer at Tyndale Seminary, Toronto, Canada.

For several years, they led groups of people in Canada and internationally using the principles and practices of collaborative theological reflection as outlined in this book.

# Notes

1. See the *Spiritual Styles Assessment* at www.TallPinePress.com

# PART I

# THEOLOGICALLY REFLECTIVE CONVERSATIONS

## CHAPTER 1

# THEOLOGICAL REFLECTION AS DIALOGUE

---

T heological reflection is a conversation that we have within ourselves or with other people. A unique feature of conversation is that it's a dialogue, not a monologue. In monologue, one person is speaking and not involving any other voices. In dialogue, at least two voices go back and forth over a problem and inform each other about it. As an example that you may recognize in your own experience, we can dialogue internally over a conflict if we're of two minds about something—we argue with ourselves. When we dialogue within ourselves, we do so because we can present two sides of an issue we feel compelled to take into account. In dialogue with others, we allow their voices, different worldviews and experience, to inform and shape how we address and redress a problem we're trying to understand.

Conversation becomes theological as we listen and speak with God. In dialogue with other people, we learn what we think and learn from what we think so we can apply new insights to our situation. As part of the process, we sometimes find we also unlearn some things we'd always taken for granted. Those taken-for-granted thoughts or ideas are the assumptions that we use when we think or act. Theological reflection is a dialogue in which new assumptions about the nature and purposes of God, scripture, the wisdom of other believers (historic and current) and wisdom from above (James 3:17) are brought to bear on how we think and act and talk with God in prayer, always with help from the Holy Spirit, as third Person of the Trinity.

This book offers perspectives on theological reflection by stating a core belief: theological reflection is conversation that's personal as well as collaborative. It's not a monologue. The book rests on an assumption that thinking itself is dialogical, even if one person, or one voice seems to be doing all the talking. In order to learn the art of theological reflection, we first come to see that when it's working, it's effective because conversation is dialogical.

Dialogue requires a particular attitude toward God, other people, oneself and the world. This attitude lets us see others on their terms rather than through our own lenses only. Just as we're prepared to understand that God's ways and thoughts are far beyond ours, so too we must come to realize that people around us have different assumptions, experiences and ways of seeing. Theological conversation itself is one way to become more dialogical. The following section describes dialogue at its best. The rest of the book has dialogue as its centre point.

The following analysis of dialogue is adapted from Paulo Freire's book, *Pedagogy of the Oppressed* (1988). Dialogue is

- An encounter between people that takes the real world into account
- An opportunity to name the world
- An existential necessity—we're less human without dialogue
- Not a deposit or consumption of knowledge
- Not a hostile, polemical argument between two or more people
- An act of creation
- Attentiveness between two people in which they see each other as a real person.

Dialogue begins as we see that all players in a conversation have a past, present and future and have similar, ordinary (existential) problems. Dialogue has a characteristic outcome. Through it, trust develops along with listening and understanding. Both parties come to have genuine concern for each other's welfare and gain an awareness of each other as a bodily presence. As a result, dialogue rests on an intense faith in the power to make, remake, create and re-create something good between two or more people. A dialogical person chooses to believe in others in advance of being with them. Dialogue is built on hope as a central, unifying and consistent attitude.

People who know how to dialogue can be called hopists. A hopist is neither an optimist nor a pessimist. Pessimists have come to believe that nothing good will come of dialogue, or of anything else. Optimists have come to believe that everything is possible. A hopist has the courage to see that some things can be done and sets about seeing what that might be. A hopist says to pessimists that, if something is to be done, we have to be attentive to the potential in things and not dismiss them in advance. A hopist says to optimists that life is complex; there may be degrees of accomplishment in what we're trying to do.

Dialogue can't exist without hope. Hope is rooted in awareness of our incompleteness, our knowing only in part—seeing through a glass darkly—this side of heaven. Hope speaks out. In contrast, hopelessness is a form of silence and passivity. Hope moves us beyond our settled opinions to search for what's worthy and calls us to expect something good to come from our efforts. Dialogical people perceive that everyone is damaged in their humanity but are inspired to see people compassionately. They realize that the point is to try; they trust God with the outcome. Dialogue is founded on love, humility and faith. It builds mutual trust between those who engage in it and strengthens the trust we have in ourselves.

Dialogue can't exist apart from love for God, others and the world. If I don't love the world, life and other people, I won't dialogue. It can't exist in the absence of humility. Dialogical hopists aren't snobs. People can't or won't dialogue if they're elitist because it calls for engagement in the common human task of learning and acting. I can't dialogue if I treat myself as a special, exclusive case. I must recognize myself in others. I can't dialogue if I project ignorance onto others. I can't dialogue if I'm failing to perceive my own ignorance. A person won't dialogue if afraid of being displaced; self-sufficiency is incompatible with it.

During an encounter, we become more human through dialogue. But how do we learn it? Learning to dialogue in theological reflection isn't so different from learning anything else. Among educators, there's been a debate over the nature of learning. There are two traditions that speak to the question. One tradition follows Jean Piaget, a Swiss psychologist and epistemologist (1896-1980); the other tradition follows L.S. Vygotsky, a Russian psycholinguist researcher, who published *Thought and Language* in 1934.

They were contemporaries and wrote to each other, conveying their many disagreements. As one example, Piaget argued that genuine intellectual competence amounts to what an individual can do unassisted. To Piaget, learning is personal. Vygotsky argued for a fundamental feature of intelligence that includes a capacity to learn along with other people. To Vygotsky, learning is collaborative. This book takes the position that they're both right. Theological reflection is both personal and collaborative, but the two traditions require different approaches, as will become more evident in later chapters.

Piaget and Vygotsky also disagreed about the use of language in learning. Piaget thought language played no formative role in the way thinking is structured. Vygotsky thought language formed the basis for thinking itself. Again, both perspectives are valid and useful in the process of learning to reflect theologically. Each position describes something that's true about human experience even though they appear to disagree. Language learned during theological reflection offers hope for building community among a group of people that are motivated personally and collaboratively to seek God's will and know God's ways.

Christian faith is unique. It requires believers to love God, expressed through obedience to him, think for themselves—on their own and with others—and love others as they love themselves. Theological reflection allows practitioners to work simultaneously toward these complex Christian aims. At its heart, theological reflection is a humbling practice that disturbs and destabilizes. In its dissonance, painful as that seems at the time, we learn what we need to know about God, others and ourselves. Theological reflection, as dialogue, is an invitation to enter into Holy Communion with others in the drama of living a faithful life in Christ.

In summary, healthy theological reflection is learned personally and collaboratively. If Christians can't reflect personally, they'd get stuck as problems arise and no one is around for them to rely on. If they've been trained to work out theological reflection all alone, they won't be effective in situations where they have to take more than their own perspective into account, which occurs frequently in ministry. What should leaders learn to do? How can they work personally and collaboratively on issues that require theological reflection?

---

**QUESTIONS FOR REFLECTION**

Can you think of times when you've engaged in genuine dialogue? What was going on? Who were you talking with? What was the subject of your conversation? Why do you think that dialogue characterized that exchange? What would have to happen in the future for you to engage in genuine dialogue more often? Are there aspects of dialogue you feel fairly comfortable with at present? Are there aspects of dialogue that are a struggle for you? How are discussions about faith influenced by genuine dialogue?

Please make some notes on your responses to these questions.

---

## EMBEDDED AND DELIBERATIVE

In this section, we'll look at several models for theological reflection. They all seek to address the crises, dissonance and destabilizing encounters that are unavoidable in ministry. To make good use of these models, begin by selecting experiences that have disturbed you in some way because they remain unresolved for you. Write out as fully as you can an encounter with another person or people that's unresolved and still causes you pain.

As people move through theological reflection, they can come to see that disturbing events reveal their blind spots. Theological reflection invites us to consider these blind spots so that we can come to grips with what they're telling us about how we currently think about God, others and ourselves. Please work through this section with your own scenario in mind—the one you just made notes about.

The next section includes several ways of doing theological reflection by providing a visual representation that identifies how these approaches foster personal theological reflection on situations that continue to unsettle you.

In the first model, Stone and Duke, authors of *How to Think Theologically*, present theological reflection as inquiry in which faith seeks understanding.[1] It's a process of thinking about life that Christians pursue because they're called to be people of faith. Theological reflection is a craft learned over time, honed by concentration and practice, which takes into account faith, church, ministry and Christian life. The model is organized around personal, interactive, dialogical and community-related practices and processes so that during theological reflection, voices other than one's own may be heeded, debated, improved upon or set aside.

In the model, the work of theology is a matter of personalized, conversational thinking about shared convictions. Its aim is to develop the best possible understanding of the faith, which the Christian church seeks to comprehend as fully as it may. For Stone and Duke, theological reflection is a conversation that addresses the human problem of knowing God that relies on and encourages the growth of spiritual intelligence, i.e., a developed capacity to address problems that arise as finite human beings attempt to understand and commune with God. The model considers intentionally what people regard as having ultimate significance. It's a good starting point for understanding theological reflection. In what follows there's a summary of several important aspects of the approach. Following that summary, some connections are made with what's presented in later chapters of the book.

To begin with, Stone and Duke's model identifies two aspects of theological reflection: embedded theology and deliberative theology.

**Embedded theology** is a first-order theology (i.e., first-hand experience). It's a language of witness that expresses immediate and direct testimonies about the meaning of faith. Rooted in preaching, teaching and practices of the Church, it's disseminated through a local congregation and assimilated by members and adherents. Embedded theology is learned implicitly, much like the way people assimilate culture. It presents itself in automatic responses people give when they encounter a disturbance which seems like a threat against their beliefs, morals or values, or when they're challenged to express their views.

Embedded theology is communally and personally embodied, as a web of meaning, that's built over time, from various sources in one's formative years. This web of meaning generates assumptions and expectations regarding Christianity. It forms identity and guides the way people operate so that it's an important part of each member's personal worldview. In summary, *Embedded Theology*, 1) forms our assumptions about ourselves, God, other people and the world; 2) grows in a particular, situated, cultural faith setting; 3) is the ground we're standing on that supports our identity as believers; and 4) forms a personal worldview.

The second aspect of Stone and Duke's model emerges as a consequence of thinking about what people have come to think about their own taken-for-granted assumptions.

**Deliberative theology** emerges from a process of careful reflection upon embedded theology. It's what Stone and Duke call a second-order activity (reflection on first-hand experience) that provides critical distance from what has been taken in and implicitly held to be true, i.e., the worldview in which we are embedded. Deliberative theological reflection becomes necessary if first order theology proves inadequate to address human experience in the form of doubt, surprise or crisis.

## THEOLOGICAL REFLECTION MODEL # 1

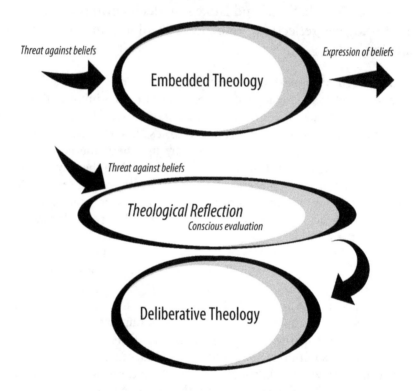

*Adapted from Howard W. Stone and James O. Duke, How to Think Theologically. (Minneapolis: Fortress Press. 1996).*

As faith seeking understanding, Stone and Duke see theological reflection as a process of reflecting upon embedded theological convictions, which leads to a deliberative theology. The process makes religious sense out of life situations once we begin to reflect on them.

Duke and Stone believe that deliberative theological reflection distances people from the personal worldview that has been forming since they were young, and raises questions such as "What do I believe? Why do I believe it?" By deliberating, believers interpret the meaning of faith and try to relate current understanding with ideas that don't easily jive with it. Deliberation assesses the adequacy of current embedded interpretations and compares them with Christian theology.

Finally, people that deliberate can evaluate the rationale and the trustworthiness of every stance. Theological reflection employs creative thinking and the whole process relies on Scripture, Tradition, Reason, and Experience. In summary, *Deliberative Theological Reflection*, 1) questions personal knowledge which has been taken for granted or assumed, 2) carries people forward when embedded theology presents them with dissonance, and 3) results in an understanding of faith that emerges from a process of reflection.

## COMMENTARY

Stone and Duke say that theological reflection is a conversation but give no specific direction for collaborative theological reflection, although they include a communal aspect of reflection. Model #1 is a visual representation of their views. Understanding the difference between embedded and deliberative theology is helpful. The model guides personal theological reflection, and the distinction between embedded and deliberative theological reflection is important to understand. Yet how might we distinguish their model from what might be called lone ranger inquiry—reflection carried out all by oneself?

In addition, it's important to make the crisis or challenge more explicit than Stone and Duke do. A disorienting situation needs to be identified as an encounter with one who is 'other'. In personal reflection, we need to recognize we're invited into dialogue with difference. This point also applies to prayer.

In prayer we address difference. We converse with one who is wholly Other. Scripture tells us that God's ways are higher than our ways. As we pray, we realize that our thinking must be shaped by that difference, that dissonance. As we open up to the possibility of dialogue, we come to see that encounters with dissonance are an opportunity for engaging another viewpoint, another person we haven't been exposed to previously, or an idea, feeling or belief about God that's new for us. An obstacle to moving forward is the feeling of fear that we might lose something essential or precious. That apprehension can hold us back. During theological reflection, it's essential to be clear with ourselves about what we might lose if we engage with difference.

## THINKING ABOUT OUR THINKING

A second model for theological reflection relies on some essentials from the first model and addresses more explicitly the role assumptions (taken-for-granted rules) play in governing thought and action. Everyone makes judgments, forms decisions and takes action based on assumptions they hold about the world. These assumptions come through experience. We take our assumptions to be true and act on them. Embedded theologies are one source for these assumptions. In critical inquiry, we stop and consider our assumptions and make them explicit: we pay attention to them because they shape our habits and expectations. Once we attend to them, we can ask whether they're the assumptions we want to continue relying on. As we reflect on our assumptions, potential losses to personal faith identities must be acknowledged and addressed.

Theological reflection doesn't necessarily lead to discarding our assumptions. The aim is to reshape assumptions into new insights that integrate what we've been taking for granted into what we're learning from God. We do this spiritual work because we see that there's something new we want to take on board as followers of Jesus Christ.

In the second model, James and Evelyn Whitehead, authors of *Method in Ministry*, offer a picture of theological reflection that seems to incorporate personal and collaborative inquiry.[2]

## THEOLOGICAL REFLECTION MODEL #2

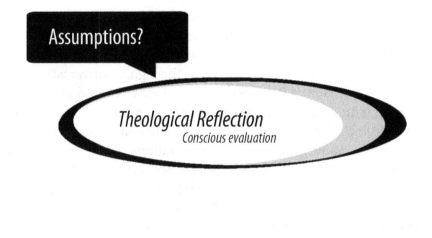

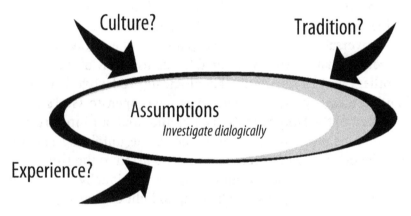

*Adapted from James D Whitehead and Evelyn E Whitehead, Method in Ministry: Theological Reflection and Christian Ministry (rev. ed.). (New York: Sheed and Ward, 1995.)*

In this model, culture, tradition and personal experience are brought to bear on assumptions that surface during theological reflection. The model depicts inquiry that takes account of important aspects of a destabilizing event. Whiteheads' approach provides an opportunity for individuals and churches to work collaboratively as they describe their personal experience, although the role of the Holy Spirit needs to be made more explicit.

During the praxis of theological reflection (i.e., union of thought, feeling and action), the Holy Spirit participates. Theological reflection unites thought, feeling and action as people investigate an event or issue through a conversation we have with ourselves (an internal dialogue), with God and/or by talking with others. Conversing—the speech act itself—is a form of action. Under favorable conditions conversing enables people to think about their thinking. Talking establishes new opportunities for thinking and acting; action clarifies talk.

Theological reflection blends thinking, feeling and acting in a way that helps people bring God's Word, will and ways to bear on troubling problems. When we reflect theologically with someone who needs us to listen to them, the Holy Spirit is Advocate, Guide and Teacher to the whole process (John 15: 26-16:15). In conversation, attention is paid to the Holy Spirit as conversational partner who enables us to listen more carefully to others and to ourselves. Theologically reflective listening is like intercessory prayer—with eyes wide open to God's mercy. We listen to the Holy Spirit's urgings and hold our interpretation of someone else's story accountable to the unfolding narrative that the other person offers to us. As we listen to the Holy Spirit, the other person and to ourselves, we continually correct our interpretation of what we're hearing in light of hearing what the other is really saying.

## COMPETING EXPECTATIONS

Model #3 differs from the Stone/Duke Model and takes Whiteheads' elaborations in a different direction. Model #3 (*Bellous and Brazeau*) focuses on situations in which competing expectations arise from a critical incident. The Model works with situations in which someone is caught in a dilemma and must decide between different ways of being faithful to God. In Model #3, we bring scripture to bear on each way of being faithful that's raised by the critical incident.

To understand how it works, suppose you're engaged in a conflict over social drinking. In beginning to engage theologically, Model #3 shows that people have expectations built on embedded theologies they read into scripture. Each side of the debate appeals to scripture as a justification for the position taken. The Model is useful because it points out that we must choose how to interpret what God requires by noticing assumptions (expectations) on each side of the dilemma. The tension in Model #3 is intense; there seems to be two legitimate paths to take. In the end, people must decide on the action to be taken.

Note that each side of the dilemma presents a combination of culture and scripture. On one side, someone is familiar with a particular cultural perspective that's typically derived from embedded theology and that seems congruent with scripture. On the other side, those involved encounter a cultural perspective, held to be equally valid by someone else, which is foreign to them. For good reasons, supported by scripture, there's a competition between the two sides of the issue. Decisions must be taken due to the critical incident.

Suppose a church is planning a fund raising event to support the acquisition of their new organ. The event is open to the whole city. As an outcome of planning the event, one group believes that having wine at the event is desirable because they think consuming alcohol is harmonious with a scripture-based way of life. As one example, they point out that Jesus turned water into wine at a wedding. The second group believes scripture forbids drinking because there are biblical prescriptions about strong drink.

Each side gives consideration to those who struggle with alcoholism but one group has the view that alcohol is acceptable; the other holds that no alcohol should be consumed. Both groups rely on scripture. For example, verses that refer to eating meat offered to idols (1 Corinthians 8:1-13) say that Christians should moderate their behavior on the behalf of weaker brothers and sisters. Using Model #3, they realize they're operating with different assumptions about what it means to be a weaker brother or sister. Each group identifies different behavior as fitting into weak and strong categories.

**THEOLOGICAL REFLECTION MODEL #3**

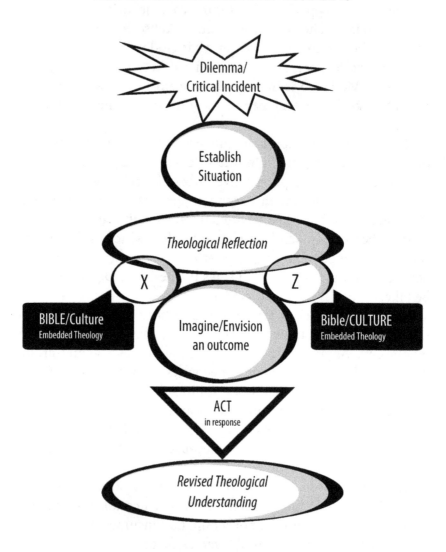

*(Bellous and Brazeau, 2001)*

Those who refuse alcohol see those who consume as weak and themselves as strong because they're strong enough to refuse.

Those who consume alcohol see those who refuse as weak and themselves as strong because they drink with a clear conscience. Each side can be supported with scripture. The disagreement is cultural and interpretive. Yet in healthy dialogue, members of each group must take account of three conditions mentioned earlier: love and obey Jesus Christ (1 Pet. 2b), think for themselves, for example, as followers did in the debate over circumcision (Acts 15:1-29) and love one another. (John 15:17)

Loving Jesus doesn't imply blind obedience. Following him isn't a holiday from personal responsibility. We must critically consider how to act, given our environment. Model #3 relies on dialogue for its success. Dialogue, with help from the Holy Spirit, enables people to distinguish what's essential to faithful living from what's non-essential.

Theological Reflection Model #3 implies a level of collaboration in order to repair conflict that may have arisen during the planning for this event. Two groups that disagree about alcohol first come to see that their assumptions differ, their experience is different and they bring different expectations to the biblical text. They may or may not be able to agree about what to do at the fundraiser, but they will gain insight into their own worldviews by using Model #3. Further, a decision must be made about what action to take for the event.

*Perspective X* focuses on **Bible** and Culture: From this perspective, people believe that scripture is clear. They assume they're interpreting it correctly. They believe the current cultural context has (or should have) minimal impact on the way they perceive what action to take concerning the critical incident.

*Perspective Z* focuses on Bible and **Culture**: From this perspective, people believe culture, history and the human condition are having too little influence on their response to the critical incident. They believe scriptural principles are authoritative, but, as an example, think scripture doesn't give clear guidelines for the critical incident. They insist that current cultural contexts and biblical texts require exegesis and should have significant impact on resolving what to do about the event.

Let's use another example to see how Model #3 works. Suppose a young man discovers that his fiancé is pregnant and he knows the child isn't his. By using Model #3, he identifies his confusion and represents the problem by naming cultural and scriptural issues on each side of his dilemma. His inner conversation clarifies decisions that need to be made, with help from Christ's example, biblical study, Christian tradition, other believers and the Holy Spirit. Model #3 calls on him to discern the following aspects surrounding his choice.

### THEOLOGICAL REFLECTION MODEL #3: THE PROCESS

#### STEP 1: ESTABLISH THE SITUATION

- Clearly state the critical incident as fully as he can

- Identify what makes it confusing, uncomfortable or destabilizing for him

- Name competing actions: 1. Break off the relationship 2. Marry her (raise the child?)

- Identify assumptions that support each of the competing actions

- Work with bible passages, images, parables, events or instances that come to mind

- Name cultural issues that arise when each action is considered

#### STEP 2: IMAGINE/ENVISION

- Name possible actions that could be taken

- List plausible outcomes of taking each of the competing actions

- Ask what would happen if he took either of these actions? Consider personal, communal, biblical and spiritual outcomes of taking the actions.

- As he imagines taking these actions, he suspends his perspective to enter empathetically into assumptions and worldview of his fiancé. He listens carefully. He reconsiders assumptions, lists fears and identifies losses and benefits. He considers as many aspects as possible of taking each of the competing actions.

**STEP 3: ACT**

- In the end, the young man must choose: not to decide is to decide. The action he takes is based on his true and best reasons and can be reconciled with carefully reading scripture and time spent in prayer. The action will express love for and obedience to God, is characterized by thinking critically (thinking about thinking) and by love for others.

Based on reflection and action, people gain new theological understanding. They situate new theological understanding in a revised pattern for thinking about the issue as a whole and take stock of losses incurred during the process. This revision comes through careful study and the courage to act in accordance with sincerely held beliefs. The revision may be an actual change of perspective or may affirm an earlier position by adding new insight.

This process may be based on personal or collaborative theological reflection. Evidence that effective theological reflection has occurred is expressed in new insight and awareness of one's true and best reasons for taking a specific action, based in scripture, prayer, one's faith tradition and the work of the Holy Spirit. The outcome is a trustworthy sense of the right thing to do.

## TYPES OF CRITICAL THEOLOGICAL INQUIRY

As already mentioned, there are two types of critical theological inquiry: personal and collaborative.

**Personal Inquiry** is an acquired ability to catch ourselves acting and thinking in certain ways. After we catch ourselves, we assess whether we want to continue in exactly the same manner. Personal reflection is something we do by ourselves as we engage in an internal dialogue. There's a significant body of literature focused on models for personal theological reflection.

**Collaborative Inquiry** is an acquired ability to reflect with others on what we're thinking and doing that helps us consider how we want to act in the future. A critical incident may be personal or communal, so that the action to be taken is individual or collective but it's a real dilemma. Collaborative reflection invites us to converse with other people in the midst of the dilemma while we're still confused and disoriented by it. The literature that helps to structure collaborative theological reflection is quite limited.

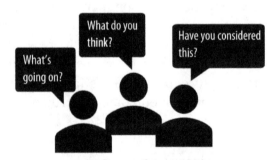

With respect to both types of inquiry, it's more challenging to reflect collaboratively, yet it also offers a rich sense of how to become a reflective practitioner. Collaborative reflection is not foreign. It's experienced around the dinner table as people try to understand a destabilizing event. In healthy table talk, family members or friends bring the three-step process outlined above to bear on a critical incident. In collaborative reflection, everyone identifies the way they perceive the critical incident in which action needs to be taken and names their previous or current experience with something that's similar to the incident from their own experience as they talk together about what action could/should be taken. Everyone...

- Speaks and listens to establish the field
- Fully describes the problem as they see it based on their own experience
- Articulates their particular perspective on the dilemma's meaning
- Helps to identify a significant theme or direction in it
- Interprets the problem so everyone moves along in understanding it
- Imagines/envisions some possible actions that could be taken
- Considers fully what might happen if the actions are taken
- Participates in evaluating the actions that are suggested

At the end, it may be that one person or more than one person takes the action that seems most congruent with living Christianly based on collaborative theological reflection.

Collaborative reflection is a conjoint educational activity. It differs from personal reflection. Christians need to be effective at personal and collaborative theological reflection since both types have limitations. For example, during personal theological reflection, we may fail to effectively check thought and action; we may be defensive rather than self-aware. As we consider the critical incident, our potential losses may overwhelm our ability to seriously consider doing the right thing. We may be self-absorbed rather than self-observing—and we may get sidetracked.

Collaborative reflection also has dangers. We may be so

engrossed with making other people happy, or minimizing conflict with them, that we fail to stand up for what God is calling us to do personally. We can be so moved by a passion for agreement that we only say what everyone else wants to hear.

At their best, collaborative and personal inquiry work effectively together to reveal blind spots in personal reflection and limit the misuse of social power in collaborative reflection. These two forms of inquiry are the groundwork for conversations that, if well carried out, create Godly, wise, liberated theological thought and action and encourage faith maturity.

### COMMENTARY

In seeing how Model #3 works, note that blind spots and dissonance characterize our social interaction as we talk together or within ourselves. In personal reflection, we clearly identify how we currently understand each side of the critical incident. In collaboration, dissonance is addressed and resolved while we talk together so that each side now comprehends the meaning that the other side holds. Resolving dissonance is different than simply coming to an agreement. The purpose of Model #3 is to acknowledge that there are at least two legitimate, biblically sound ways to see a problem. During dialogue in Model #3, two sides may agree or agree to disagree but if the legitimacy of each side is clearly understood, they can remain engaged with one other in a trusting Christian community.

The role of dissonance is central to moving forward in theological reflection. As we try to collaborate by using Model #3, we see blind spots in our own thinking by acknowledging that the meaning on the other side makes no sense at first. These conversations are typified by conflict sparked by the different points of view inherent on each side of the debate. As we realize the value and meaning of the other side, conflict is an opportunity to notice our own blind spots and to do something about them.

The roles of dissonance and blind spots are discussed more

fully in later chapters, but the following sections pick up the idea of dissonance in order to show that healthy theological reflection affirms some aspects of our thinking and talking together and refines other aspects. Through a healthy process we learn what's really on our hearts. Jesus said, "Out of the overflow of the heart the mouth speaks." (Matthew 12:34b) What's really on our hearts has an impact on what we do.

### A FAITHFUL PRACTICE THAT HELPS US SHIFT OUR GROUND

Theologically reflective conversations allow us to perceive the state of our own heart and identify insights that arise through self-observation. As we experience conversation, something can shift in our understanding of God, others and ourselves. Theological conversation invites change. This belief is based on the view that changes in our own perspectives arise from lived experience—something happens that just doesn't fit what we've always thought. If we are de-stabilized we feel as if we can no longer stand our ground or at least, we wonder if we can continue to think and act as we have been doing.

A life of faith is moved forward by perceiving blind spots in our thinking and by allowing the dissonance that shows up to reveal what we need to surrender to God in order to be more mature as followers of Jesus. Shifts in our perception can arise through the practice of traditional Christian disciplines and *Lectio Divina* is one example. It's a historic practice and was central to devotional life in Eastern and Western Christianity. Its benefits are indisputable. The most common form of *Lectio Divina* is outlined in the next section.

Please take time to work through the practice using a scriptural passage that's significant to you. When we begin to perceive how and why we do what we do, our implicit knowledge is moved by that insight. The shift, slight as it may be, allows us to know God, others and ourselves more fully: we come to taste and see that God is good.

### EXERCISE: LECTIO DIVINA

In *Lectio Divina*,[3] each stage invites you to read a selected passage of scripture and meditate on it in different ways. Find a place where you're alone and mentally, emotionally relaxed. Clear the time in your schedule to be uninterrupted for at least 30 minutes. As you become familiar with the method, you'll settle on a length of time that best suits you. Before you begin, calm your mind, spirit and body. You may do this by breathing deeply and clearing your mind of all pressures and concerns. Relax tension in your body by being conscious of each part individually. Sit in a comfortable position. Every once in a while, remind yourself about your posture and remind yourself to breathe deeply.

*Lectio* (Using the senses to perceive: *Sensing*)

*Read the passage of scripture.* Sacred reading begins by listening to the words you're looking at on the page. Read slowly enough to allow them to sink in, quickly enough to keep from being distracted. Ancient Christians attributed eagerness to this first reading. There's something here you want to sense. It's reverential reading. As you focus on the text, and, because you have set aside time to be with God, there may be tears as you read. Let them come. Deep emotion was closely connected with *Lectio Divina*. Don't try to understand why you weep. Let emotion enrich your devotional encounter with the words of scripture.

You're listening for the voice of God: a still, small voice that beckons to you from the text. Remember to breathe freely, sitting with a relaxed but not slumped posture. Be attentive to the atmosphere of the passage. Be fully present to it. Imagine what it would be like to be there. Picture the landscape, people, immediate surroundings and climate. Sit quietly.

Think about those involved in the passage. What do you learn about them from the story? Use as many senses as possible to engage the story and make it come alive for you. Is there anyone in the passage who is something like you? This isn't a time to think about what the text means but what you sense in it. Right now, you're not responsible to bring the text's meaning to anyone else. This time is for you. Listen for God as you read. To hear God speak, remain silent. Quiet yourself. Listen for a word, phrase, image or sensation that stands out. Reverential reading is harder for some than others. Get curious. Relax. See what happens.

*Meditatio* (Using cognition to ruminate: *Remembering*)

*Read the passage again*, this time ask yourself 'why' questions. Consider its meaning and significance. This time is for thinking that's more like ruminating or chewing on what you've found. Why were those particular words or images included? Why was it written in this way? What's being taught? If you're having difficulty finding meaning in the passage, try pretending to be a character you can identify with, or all the characters. What do you already know about this sort of person or these sorts of people? How does that knowledge inform your reading? Your goal is to understand its meaning based on what you already know and have already experienced.

Thinking is about the past. We think about what we already know. Try to gather your thoughts from past experience and associations. What do you know about this text? What do you wonder about it? What does it remind you of? How is one phrase, image or idea linked to another? Does any word or image remind you of another passage of scripture? Don't look it up now. Just try to remember. What are your questions? Write them down.

What's a main point or lesson that you can take away from the text? What's it about? Take some of the ideas and ponder them, as Mary did, after Jesus was born and the angels and shepherds came to celebrate his birth. (Luke 2:19)

*Memorize an aspect of the passage* and let it sink in. Let the words touch and affect you at a deep level so that what you read is personal. Welcome God's words into your life and allow these signs (black marks on a page) to be living words—a message from God in which God is present. It's at this point that you might say: Oh I see! I get it! That's what it's about. Focus on the words of scripture. What do they add to scripture that's already in your heart?

*Oratio* (Using emotion to respond: *Feeling*)

At this point, the reader invites feeling and thinking to be united in prayer. It was through the Rule of St Benedict that Anselm received the practice of *Lectio Divina*. He shaped the practice. To him, it was a way into prayer through meditative reading "with the aim of purity of heart and compunction of tears" so that continual "meditation may finally impregnate your soul and form it in its own image."[4] As you *read the passage for the third time*, talk to God. Consider how the passage affects you emotionally.

What are you feeling? There are no incorrect feelings. As you pray, tell God your feelings. Again, feelings are based on what you've already thought, experienced and understood.

Becoming emotionally intelligent, so that we sense what we feel and how it influences thought and action, is hard work. Feelings become more evident as you continue to read. Let your feelings open up the passage to your understanding. Only rarely are people really good at easily naming their feelings. If you're typically someone who doesn't know or shuts down on feelings, recall your posture and your breathing as you try to sense your feelings.

As you regain a comfortable position and breathe freely, perhaps you might lay your hands on your knees or in your lap in an open gesture to signal you want to understand yourself, as God understands you, in particular because of what this passage touches in you. To do this emotional work you need help from the Holy Spirit. Let the Spirit remind you of Jesus so that you're comfortable doing the spiritual and emotional work of crying out to God.

The medieval person was comfortable with the weeping that also might occur at this point. Scripture, particularly the psalms, makes it clear that God wants us to cry out to Him. God hears the cries of the heart—of this we can be sure. Scripture says God records our tears in a bottle—they are precious to God. (Psalm 56:8) At this point, our prayer may include four elements: Adoration, Confession, Thanksgiving and Supplication (ACTS).

There's often passionate prayer during this reading that draws us toward the heart of God. We offer what's on our heart to God so that God, who is the lover of our souls, can gaze on that offering. In this act, what we know about God is touched compassionately by what God knows of us, and by the Good that God wants for our lives. Don't be troubled if you don't feel anything or don't feel anything deeply. Simply tell God honestly what's going on within you. Sit quietly for a period of time.

*Contemplatio* (Using intuition to internalize: *Appropriating*)

The *final reading of the text* encourages contemplation. Many of us associate contemplation with religions other than Christianity, but we're forgetting our history. Contemplation requires us to be quiet and still in contrast to the normal pace of life. We're so driven by activity and noise that remaining still and quiet can be difficult, particularly if we travel with cell phones and ear phones that are hooked to media in the outside world. Silence itself may feel very foreign. You need patience to wait for your ordinary distractions to calm down. Focus on the sounds of silence.

Contemplation requires us to focus on an inner world. Now is the time to consider more fully the previous three readings and internalize them. At this point, you assimilate words you have been reading and considering. This involves nothing more than sitting quietly to listen and receive. First concentrate on your breathing. Is it steady? Is it natural? Focus on what your heart is telling you. Notice feelings and thoughts. What comes to your mind? Can you observe anything in these thoughts that leads you back to the passage? Return to a state of openness and expectation. You may feel anxious, bored or frustrated. Simply tell God what you're feeling, make no excuses. Ask for help. Close your eyes. If you find you don't receive any insight, return to the words of scripture.

To contemplate, allow yourself to enter into quiet, centering peacefulness. Christians have described the practice as attentiveness, which involves giving full and uncluttered attention to something. That's all you are being asked to do. Become aware of any mental chatter and tell it to go away. Now is not the time for being preoccupied with anything other than what God is saying from the text.

This is Christian meditation. We don't enter into this practice to find absolute silence, the absence of all thought or emptiness, as many Eastern religions do. We enter into quiet conversation to hear, and learn to hear, the voice of God. We enter into conversation with God. The conversation can become dialogical; it's rooted and grounded in our experience of God and Jesus Christ as revealed through Holy Scriptures, by the Holy Spirit and within the heritage of the faithful.

As we enter into meditation, how we conceive of God matters a very great deal. If God is a frightening or frustrating Presence, due to personal experiences, this part of *Lectio Divina* can be painful. Be encouraged. Through this practice, and particularly its expanded version, we can come to hear God as the Living God longs to be revealed to us, as lover of our souls. As we relieve ourselves of distraction, in conversation, we learn what God is really like.

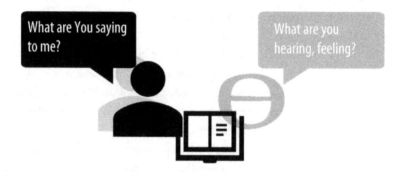

It's hard to contemplate if duties, thoughts or people clutter our thought life. Tell yourself that right now isn't the time for fretting over these issues. Tell yourself that right now you can solve none of the problems that trouble you. God offers you undivided attention right now and will be with you later as you try, with renewed strength and wisdom, to tackle problems and opportunities when the time is right to pay attention to them.

So much of the time people say: don't just stand (sit) there, do something! Now you can say to yourself: don't just do something, sit here. Breathe comfortably and deeply. If you let God in now, later you'll be able to give other people and your projects your undivided attention. You'll be better at doing it. You'll gain new insight about being attentive to others if you give full attention to God now. At the end of the time period you established for your sacred reading, close your meditation.

# Notes

1. Howard Stone and James Duke, *How to Think Theologically*, Minneapolis: Fortress Press, 1996.

2. James D Whitehead and Evelyn E Whitehead, *Method in Ministry:*

*Theological Reflection and Christian Ministry* (rev. ed.), Sheed and Ward, 1995.

3. The following descriptions are informed by the following sources: Corinne Ware, *Discover Your Spiritual Type* (An Alban Institute Publication, 1995); Michael and M.C. Norrisey, *Prayer and Temperament* (Charlottesville, Virginia: The Open Door Inc., 1991), and St. Anselm.

4. Benedicta Ward, Trans, Ed., *The Prayers and Meditations of St. Anselm* (Hamondsworth, Middlesex, England: Penguin Books, 1973), 45.

CHAPTER 2

# PRACTICING HEALTHY THEOLOGICAL
# REFLECTION

hapter One presents three models for theological reflection—all of which are useful. In all cases, theological reflection is conversation that can lead to dialogue. If it does, it's marked by drama, investment and conflict. Even if people disagree, through the process, they have access to insights about what's central to faith and what's peripheral to it. Chapter One also introduced the idea of personal blind spots. If theological reflection is well done, it's hard spiritual work that uncovers assumptions (that can be blind spots) we've always relied upon. Healthy theological reflection invites us to question whether we want these assumptions to continue directing how we think and act.

When theological reflection becomes dialogue, something happens that complicates our attempt to live superficially with other believers: we tell each other the truth. In so doing, we gain access to our true and best reasons for the ways we behave. During that process, we may reveal blind spots in our own way of seeing God, others, Christianity and ourselves. One way to deal with blind spots is to exercise spiritual practices in a loving environment. In these practices, we're provided with an opportunity to tell the truth, pray, study scripture, live in a worshipping community and intentionally build spiritual friendships. Spiritual practices affirm our capacity to use healthy reason so that we're aware of our true and best reasons for why we think and act the way we do. As we do spiritual work, our links with the Living God, other people and ourselves are strengthened.

Perhaps the first chapter made dialogue sound easy. It isn't. This chapter explores its complexity. The purpose of this chapter is to outline how healthy versus unhealthy reason plays out in theological reflection as it's exercised during conversation. Reason itself is central in all the activities that offer support for theological reflection. Healthy reason is best described as "a peculiarly stubborn effort to think clearly" about something.[1] Jesus used reason in this sense when the Pharisees' claimed that he was relying on Beelzebub to cast out demons. He replied to their accusation with his strong man argument.[2]

In order to expand on the complexity reason brings to conversation, two practices are outlined in the next section. These practices (Focusing and Artful Listening) include a description of unhealthy reason that will always hinder dialogue. That hindrance arises because unhealthy reason violates the sense of felt connection among a group of people or between two people. A sense of felt connection, which is a definition of the human side of spirituality,[3] is essential for dialogue to flourish. After these two practices are outlined, there's a description of the trajectory of reason that helps to see more clearly the fullness of reason that's available to Christians as they reflect theologically. The last section introduces the Latin term Sapience and outlines it's role in practising healthy theological reflection.

## FOCUSING

If we continue to define it as a peculiarly stubborn effort to get clear about something, we can more easily note reason's centrality in theological reflection. In addition, we can begin to see how reason plus telling the truth establishes and maintains that sense of felt connection that matters to us as we work towards making conversation more dialogical.

In terms of spiritual connection during theological reflection, it's also true that the human spirit (the communicative agency that allows us to have a sense of felt connection) is our link to the

Holy Spirit and to effective connection with other people. That sense of felt connection nurtures and supports faith through self-observation. When considering what it means to say that spirituality is a sense of felt connection, it helps to understand and use a secular practice that American psychologist Eugene Gendlin noticed in his clients.[4] Because of the way it works, as we understand and experience it, focusing helps us to improve our ability to reflect theologically.

Gendlin called the practice "focusing." He discovered it by asking why some people recover with psychological treatment and others don't. He analyzed client interviews to uncover what people do to benefit from treatment. He noted that clients who benefitted were able to focus even before their sessions started. He isn't dismissive of psychological treatment, but thinks that focusing is what enables clients to recover, not psychology or psychiatry alone. He also believes focusing can be learned. In focusing, clients spend time investigating what Gendlin called a "felt sense" of something.

To explain focusing further, spirituality as a felt sense of connection is useful. As felt connection, spirituality describes biological, cultural, sociological, neurological and psychological dimensions of becoming a human being. The sense of felt connection that emerges through these five ordinary human processes is what allows an individual to focus on a felt sense in the way that Gendlin described. Focusing invites someone to pay full attention to the embodied way they think and feel about something that matters to them. As they focus, people sift through their awareness of what's on their mind and get a better sense of what it means to them. When focusing works well, we become aware of our true and best reasons for the ways we act and think and we have an opportunity to ask ourselves if these are the ways we want to continue thinking and acting.

Like focusing, in the models described in chapter one, theological reflection is a way of thinking that sifts through thought and feeling until we get clear about something that's bothering us because it's destabilized us in some way. In James 1:12-15, scripture talks about aspects of that process in a particular way that implies we need to pay attention to our thought life and the motion of our own souls.

> Blessed are those who persevere under trial, because when they have stood the test, they will receive the crown of life that God has promised to those who love him. When tempted, no one should say, 'God is tempting me.' For God cannot be tempted by evil, nor does he tempt anyone; but each of you is tempted when, by your own evil desire, you are dragged away and enticed. Then, after desire has conceived, it gives birth to sin; and sin, when it is full-grown, gives birth to death....Submit yourselves, then, to God. Resist the devil, and he will flee from you. Come near to God and he will come near to you. (James 1:12-15:4:7-8a)

Focusing involves picking out patterns that get in the way of paying attention to our thought life, which is helpful for those who long to hear God's voice. There are similarities between focusing and theological reflection that help us understand what gets in the way of self-observation, interferes with telling ourselves the truth, and intimidates our confidence as we try to tell the truth to other people.

That hindrance is unhealthy reason. By identifying the limits of reason, we see connections among faith, reason and theological reflection. Theological reflection links faith and reason in a way that encourages faith maturity if reason is properly understood, since its true function is to attain to the truth or supreme good,[5] not to turn people into skeptics. For followers of Jesus, to know is to know God. The proper use of reason is to see it as a servant in that effort, not our master, as many modern secular theorists wanted people to believe during the last century.

### THE PRACTICE OF FOCUSING

To apply focusing to theological reflection is to take scripture as the starting point, e.g., James 1:12-15 quoted earlier. Theological reflection allows us to pay attention and actively observe what's in our hearts as we read scripture—as it also reads us. Christians find renewal by thinking theologically and living integrous lives—by aligning what's in the heart with how they act in the world. Transformation is the outcome: we're transformed by watching the movement of our own souls as we come face to face with the Living God, during the study of scripture, prayer and in community with other believers who are involved in the same process of formation.

Focusing helps to understand how theological reflection works. In focusing, you commit to spend at least one half hour by yourself or with another person to get clear about something that's important yet puzzling. It may be something that showed up in scripture or a situation you want scripture to speak into. Focusing is the first step in hearing what the situation means to you.

Make sure you feel relaxed and safe. You want to get a felt sense about the problem. You want to find out all that's involved in it. A felt sense is a large, vague feeling, layered with thought and feeling but isn't merely a feeling. A felt sense unites mind, heart and body in awareness that profoundly influences your life because it's been shaped by personal experience. It's an embodied, internal sense encompassing everything you know about the subject, situation or problem. A felt sense tends to communicate itself all at once, with all its complexity, rather than giving us detail by detail.

Think of a felt sense as tasting something you can't quite describe, or perhaps, the sense you have when you listen to music by giving your full attention to it. A felt sense makes a powerful impact: it's 'a big round unclear experience'.[6] Speaking to another person (a witness) as you focus helps to realize what's going on in a felt sense as it's unpacked and its elements and contradictions are laid out.

The body is something like a computer. Experience is stored on a hard drive. When we speak the truth in love, we're trying to access what's stored in memory so that we can make sense of it. Speaking the truth in love is a pleasant feeling: you say and hear all that you've experienced about something. At the end, you feel released from confusion about what's involved in that felt sense. You learn something new—or see what you've known about it, seemingly for the first time. A felt sense isn't just what you think or feel. It's both together. In addition, as you focus, you resist unhealthy reason. In focusing, you create a friendly environment for yourself. The process of focusing involves the following steps.

---

**STEPS IN FOCUSING**

*Clearing a space.* Ask yourself what it is that you feel about the problem you selected. When a concern comes, don't go inside it. Stand back. Say, yes, there it is. See it from a distance but remain close enough to see clearly.

*Asking:* what's the main thing right now about all that's involved? Usually there are several things that come into view.

*Having a felt sense*. Select one problem or aspect of it. Pay attention. Again, don't go into it. Keep a bit of distance. Visualize that you are present to but not inside the problem. Ask: what does all this feel like? What is my body conveying to me? Are you carrying tension somewhere in your body? Try to release that tension by paying attention to it. What is the tension like? Is it sharp? Is there pain? Are your muscles cramped? Again, let yourself feel the unclear sense of all that (the troubling issue)....

*Getting a handle*. What is the quality of the unclear sense? What word, phrase, posture, image, impression, action comes to mind? Stay with it until a word feels, or words feel, just right.

*Resonating*: Go back and forth between the felt sense and word or words you chose to describe it. Check how they resonate with each other. See if there is a little bodily signal that lets you know there's a fit (e.g., a sigh, easier breathing). The felt sense and the word or words must work with each other and connect. As you resonate with a felt sense, let words you use change if the fit doesn't seem to work.

*Asking:* What is it about the whole problem that makes up the quality, word(s) chosen? Sense it again, freshly, vividly. When it's there, tap it, touch it—be with it. Ask what makes the whole problem so [word chosen]. What is the worst of it? What does it need? What would it feel like to be okay? Wait a while. Be patient with these questions until a slight shift occurs in your body and/or your mind.

*Receiving*: Accept what comes, even if it's a slight release. Remain with it for a while. There will be other times to try again. Don't depend only on one

---

time sitting with a felt sense to make a decision about what you should do about it. Set another time or other times to go over the experience again to see if you have the same or a similar outcome.

A felt sense reveals itself in a friendly environment as someone listens compassionately. In a safe place, we expose a truth without wanting to cover it up. What we uncover interests us and speaking about it relieves a burden we've been carrying because of its affects on us.

As we reflect, we become curious, not defensive. During focusing, refuse to misuse reason. Unhealthy reason can't help free you from the trap you feel caught in. Reason is misused if we employ the following ways of talking and thinking about other people or ourselves.

Unhealthy reason draws us into thinking in the following ways, which include:

- Belittling the problem

- Analyzing it by grabbing at reasons that effectively dismiss it as a real problem

- Blaming someone else or getting stuck on someone else's part in the situation

- Suppressing the problem by 'gritting our teeth and bearing it'

- Lecturing ourselves about how stupid we are to take it seriously

- Drowning in the feelings attached to the problem

We engage unhealthy reason if we pretend the problem isn't serious and has a simple solution, or that it means we're worthless, hopeless and alone. If we're immersed in unhealthy reason, we hear the voice of a skeptic who accuses us through mockery, by giving us what sounds like reason but that has the power to keep us from being courageous enough to seek God.

If we give in to unhealthy reason, we remain alone. While we're drowning in the mental chatter of unhealthy reason, we can't believe God's love is available.

## SUMMARY

Read through the description of focusing. As you begin to carry it out, you'll need to find a comfortable, quiet place in order to create the right environment. The exercise refers to finding a partner, a witness, but also suggests you may carry it out alone. Having a witness is a profoundly renewing experience but witnesses need to clearly understand their role. The following section on the practice of Artful Listening outlines that role. It's essential for a witness to follow the Artful Listening instructions. Success in focusing depends on freeing yourself from unhealthy reason; witnesses must not introduce it either.

As people focus, healthy reason makes it possible to mature into the fullness of God. It aids us in knowing God and Jesus Christ, with the Holy Spirit's help, (John 14:15-27) on the basis of what we already know about them. As a way of knowing, it's not merely mental knowledge; it includes intimacy and friendship (John 15:14-15) and helps us understand what's in our own hearts. In focusing, it's essential to notice when you're using healthy versus unhealthy reason. During your practice, as you pay attention to your own thought, consider the patterns of unhealthy reason that are described above and speak back to them in a way that conforms to the truth that God loves you and that you're worthy of God's love.

## THE PRACTICE OF ARTFUL LISTENING

In his book on focusing, Gendlin describes the kind of listening that someone needs from another person if they invite that person to witness their act of focusing.[7] If we focus with another person, that individual acts as a witness to our process. Witnesses learn to listen well. In Artful Listening, derived from Gendlin's suggestions, a witness offers full attention to the one who's focusing. The task is to indicate whether the witness can follow what the speaker is saying. Witnesses are trying to hear what another person feels/thinks/embodies about a problem or situation. Embodied feeling and thinking are united in a felt sense as the focuser explores what he or she is trying to convey.

---

#### STEPS IN ARTFUL LISTENING

As the one who is focusing speaks, after a few sentences, witnesses might say, for example:

- Yes

- I see

- I realize this is important to you

- Would you say a bit more about…

- Can you tell me a story about that….

What matters is that focusers sense they're really being heard. Whatever witnesses choose to say, it must arise out of genuinely paying attention. As they listen, they put nothing of themselves into the conversation. They tell the speaker the truth. If they say that they follow what the one focusing is saying, this must be true. They also say clearly and kindly when they aren't yet following. As an example, they might say something like:

- Can you say that another way? I didn't quite get it.

- Please say more? I'm a bit lost.

Witnesses never introduce topics of their own that the focuser didn't request. In other forms of speaking and listening, listeners discern what of their experience is relevant and necessary but not in Artful Listening. Never push an interpretation of what's being said. Don't mix your own ideas with what a speaker wants to convey. The only reason witnesses speak while someone is focusing is to convey their understanding of what's meant by the embodied feeling/thought. To show they understand exactly, they say back the other person's meaning. If you're a witness, you may use your own words but with particularly sensitive aspects of what the other person is saying, put the thought into the speaker's own words. If you're having trouble getting the meaning, ask for repetition and/or clarification.

There are two important mistakes that may be made in Artful Listening: talking about ourselves and not talking at all. People who are focusing need to hear you speak to realize that you get what they mean. For every 4 or 5 sentences they speak, witnesses convey in a sentence or two what they've heard. They don't fix, change or try to improve it. They try to get to the crux of what the focuser wants to convey. They feel it themselves, if they can.

Witnesses make a statement about the crux of what was said. As beginners, they're very accurate with their words. Later, when they have more practice, they may give back the crux of the embodied feeling/thought by using some of their own words, but they make sure these words accurately reflect the focuser's meaning. As they listen, witnesses

- Check out the meaning they've heard from the focuser who's speaking

- Let speakers correct the meaning and add to it, if they want to do so

- Take in what's being said, saying it back until they've stated it the way that's accepted

- Make another sentence to say what it means to them or how they feel it, if they can

- Say back, bit by bit, what the speaker means

- Don't let the speaker say more than can be taken in and said back

- Interrupt and say back what they've heard; then let the speaker go on

You know you're getting it right if speakers go further into the problem, disagree with what you're saying back, and are able to say more about what they mean. By listening, you may not get it right the first time or even the second or third time, but speakers are led by your responses to go deeper into sensing what they mean. Remember that the internal process of the one who focuses is what matters. A speaker may stop talking if

- They feel understood or they feel misunderstood, so check it out
- They need to go deeper into their own feelings/ thoughts, but aren't quite ready

When the process is going well, speakers relax, breathe more freely, say something like: Yes, that's it! When speakers are laying out a felt sense, they feel tense. The free flow of their breathing is interrupted. As they sense that they're putting into words what they really mean to say, with you as their witness, they realize they don't have to say it again. They relax. They don't have to hold the feeling/thought in the body any longer. If a speaker is quiet, relaxed, don't speak needlessly. It's a time of rest, relaxation and peace.

If speakers keep repeating the same thing, it may be they sense you haven't quite heard it yet. They need to know you've got their meaning; they need to hear that you get it.

Always check out how your words differ from the way focusers are saying what they feel/think and ask if you're getting it right. As you respond, the speaker's face may get tight, tense, confused. The speaker is trying to understand what you mean by your response. If you haven't yet conveyed that you understand in a satisfactory way:

- Stop
- Ask the person to say again how it is they feel/think

The speaker may change the subject. If that happens, he or she might have given up on getting the more personal thing right. Check it out. Say something such as:

- I'm still with you. I don't yet understand but I want to understand.
- Check your tone of voice. Is it relaxed?
- Breathe
- Think: it doesn't matter when I get this right. I will eventually. I have time.

Sometimes people may share something with a witness that is uncomfortable to hear. If you find it hard to accept what someone is saying, think of the person as struggling with the same qualities you find difficult. Whether you're following or getting lost in the process of Artful Listening, sometimes simply stop. Sense your own tangle of thoughts, feelings and needs. Clear your mind. Give attention to the speaker. Remember, you've committed to listen for an agreed on time. If you're still within that time limit and have checked out your own sensations, feelings and thoughts, return to listening carefully. If people are speaking the truth in love, and a witness is listening artfully, both people feel alert and slightly excited. They're curious about what might happen next.

### THE TRAJECTORY OF REASON

Focusing and Artful Listening help to understand how theological reflection allows people to move forward in faith maturity. Focusing describes some of what's meant by self-observation. Its practice helps clarify what pre-modern Christians may have done as they meditated on God. Focusing is more like Christian meditation than meditation in other religious traditions. For example, in general, major Eastern religions tend to teach that meditation should move people into internal silence.

Successful Eastern meditation stills and quiets internal mental chatter that clutters the mind. Meditation creates inner openness that's empty of voices, images, thoughts, impressions, so that one's inmost being becomes a place of undistracted stillness and quietness, and ideally, of complete emptiness. In contrast, Christian meditation (East and West) invites people to enter into conversation with God, although being still and calming our mental chatter are both involved.

For pre-modern Christians, practices of meditation and prayer such as *Lectio Divina* were at the heart of theological reflection and were learned from experienced practitioners. These practices weren't necessarily written down step-by-step so much as those who were skilled passed them on to others face-to-face. Like Christian meditation, focusing doesn't invite us into inner silence but into conversation that's already going on in our hearts. As a consequence, when that conversation includes God, our concept of God is central to our ability to carry out healthy theological reflection, as are personal self-concepts.

Healthy reason, as mentioned, is essential to healthy theological reflection. Because it's an invitation into conversation with God, the way we think about God is central. Examining God concepts and self-concepts in light of scripture makes theological reflection healthy. During the process, reason serves the spiritual work of self-observation. It allows us to perceive what's in our own hearts and speak into that meaning by telling the truth and using healthy reason. Reason allows us to think about our own thinking and perceive the personal meaning that shapes the way we conceive of God, other people, the world and ourselves. In order for theological reflection to be healthy, reason must not be allowed to become relentlessly skeptical. Skepticism hovers over heart and mind like a killing frost.

Theological reflection is at the core of spiritual life. Christians and faith communities don't mature without reflecting theologically. Essential to the process is a refusal to let unhealthy reason distract and confuse reflection. Focusing, described earlier, includes a summary of what's meant by unhealthy reason. A fundamental state of mind during theological reflection is the determined resistance to give in to unhealthy reason and a willingness and ability to counteract it if it does surface in our thinking, acting or speaking. The impact of unhealthy reason prevents a conversation from ever becoming dialogical.

In order to get clear about healthy reason and its role in theological reflection, there's a twentieth century shift that's essential to understand. The shift emerged in response to the philosophical investigations of reason that have characterized Western thinking since the 1700s. Immanuel Kant (1724-1804) is at the core of that shift but he didn't intend his view of reason to produce it.[8] Those who followed Kant misled the West about what he introduced into the discussion of reason. The next section outlines the path of reason and describes its impact on a major mistake that was made in the last century—a mistake that dis-privileged faithful belief and curtailed what believers think is possible as they try to use reason during theological reflection.

The shift in question has two strands that denigrated theological reflection. With the first, spun through myths introduced by Freud, people came to believe self-observation was nothing more than psychological. Spiritual practices lost value and power in their historical claim to provide a link to a God who offers consolation and protection. Christians fail to realize what was lost if psychology has the only role in self-observation. Revitalizing theological reflection requires getting past worrying whether spiritual work is psychology and realizing that spiritual self-observation renews unity between knowing, being and doing as we become mature believers—a promise ancient believers took on faith.

To pick out the second strand, we must investigate aspects of what it means to know anything at all. Theological reflection is a way of knowing (and coming to know) that's similar to other ways. It's also different. Jesus defined eternal life as knowing God and himself, whom God has sent (John 17:3). Modernity appeared to make this sort of knowing foolish, if not impossible. Yet, if we recall more ancient views of reason that didn't fall prey to modern prejudice, we uncover the richness of a tradition that relies on healthy reason.

To understand how healthy reason functions, we're well advised to consider the ancient world's nuanced ways of describing human thought. There was a tendency to divide the power of thinking into two broad categories, reason and intuition, a division the ancient Greek world captured in two terms, *dianoia* or reason (διανοια) and *nous* or intuition (νους).[9]

Early in the modern period, Kant developed two German terms, *Vernunft* (reason) and *Verstand* (intuition), to signify a similar division, but one that introduced new roles for the terms. In short, Kant reversed the previous positions these terms held within Christian tradition, without intending to separate reason from its reliance on God. Yet his followers strengthened his distinction in ways that shaped twentieth century approaches to faith and science. Faith was reduced in value and was thought of an absence of reason.

To begin describing reason's trajectory, for ancient Greeks (generally) *dianoia* referred to cognitive understanding grounded on mathematics and offered explanations that guided knowledge that's pursued for its own sake. *Dianoia* is discursive thinking built up by looking around at a world of objects (including people) and seeing them as measurable. It's an activity that perceives objects and makes sense of them. Greeks used other terms to describe aspects of this 'looking around' approach, for example, *episteme* (επισταμαι), *theoria* (θεωρια), the understanding useful in producing things, *techne* (τεχνη), e.g., machines or art, and knowledge applied to conduct, *phronesis* (φρονησις).[10]

Looking around at the world provides useful knowledge. As one engineering student put it, mathematics describes the world rather well, although it has to construct a cow as a sphere and can't say much about the wind, where or how it blows. Describing the world mathematically allows us to benefit from science and medicine and supports the comfort and plenty we enjoy in the West. Yet it also privileges the material over the spiritual world and reduces humanity to what's measurable. As one consequence, *dianioa* debases objects that are supra-sensible (that can't be perceived by using the five senses). As a consequence of a modern privilege given to the five senses as the primary means for knowing anything, God was reduced to non-relevance or non-existence. This happened as modernity placed higher value on *dianoia* than *nous*, which ancient and medieval worlds didn't do.

Paired with, but distinct from *dianoia*, *nous* is received knowledge. In the past, Christians also used the Latin *intellectus* to signify knowledge that came directly from God. Even ancient Greeks had a vague sense that *nous* was somehow knowledge received through a cosmic connection that's hard to define in what they wrote about it.[11] *Nous* refers to an awareness or attentiveness in which the knower and the known confront each other directly and become identified.[12] It refers to intellect or mind; it's an activity based on looking up, not around, in order to gain knowledge of things beyond mere sight.

Intuition, in this sense, implies a way of knowing born of connection to something larger than oneself. There's a sense of Being implicit in *nous*—a sense of felt connection to the object of one's attention. In this view, people have potential to know things through *noesis* (an operation of *nous*) but attention can be distracted. One must be intentional about knowing in this sense. It seems fair to say that distractions could arise from a lack of self-awareness, self-understanding and self-regulation—disciplines that were part of training apprentices in ancient Christian traditions. Through discipline, a recipient's attentiveness becomes aware of what's on offer through *noetic* experience.

From the perspective of *nous*, intellection and meditation allow someone to receive knowledge directly from God in flashes of insight (a way of knowing Plato also prized). This knowledge is spiritually derived, based on looking upward, which pre-moderns valued more than reason used when looking around at the world. During the Medieval period, philosophical practice descending from *nous* was companion to attention paid to the motion of the soul and the continual refinement of meaning derived through experience. *Nous* was part of a foundational process required in order to make meaning from experience. It was spiritual and what we now tend to call psychological. Yet ultimately, we want to link looking up and looking around in healthy theological reflection. This is an impulse conveyed in art that's in the Vatican in Rome. There's a famous painting there called *The School of Athens* by Raphael. It depicts these two ways of knowing: looking up, exemplified by Plato, and looking around, exemplified by Aristotle.

Recall the definition of reason given earlier as 'a peculiarly stubborn effort to get clear about something'. That definition comes from Anthony Gottlieb's book, *The Dream of Reason,* which examines reason from the Pre-Socratic Greeks to the Renaissance. He makes the point that there's no such thing as Philosophy. In his view, philosophy " is more the history of a sharply inquisitive cast of mind"[13] than a specific discipline, particularly if one considers the vastness, disagreement and dissonance in the products of that cast of mind, as one looks back over the history of philosophical thought in the Western tradition. That is, the way one uses reason has a character that remains consistent, (that cast of mind, that stubborn effort to get clear about something) but the contents, ideas, produced by that cast of mind don't only differ from one another, they sharply disagree about the nature of thought, human experience, the world we can see and the world we can't see.

During the early decades of the twentieth century, that second strand in the trajectory of reason showed up, i.e., the modern privilege given to *dianoia* and *Verstand*. This strand *substituted content for the process of reason itself.* Freud is an exemplar of this second strand, but it was also congruent with the mood of the times in medicine and science. Freud took great pains to convince his wide readership in North America that the evidence people are using reason is that they no longer believe in God: unbelief was the evidence that one was using reason correctly. Rather than promoting a cast of mind that creates particular content, and does so by the stubborn effort to get clear about something, Freud, and atheism generally, asserted that unbelief is the only trustworthy evidence that people were making good use of reason: to many twentieth century atheists, maturity is achieved by taking up unbelief.

But Freud made a fundamental mistake about how reason operates. He mistook the content of thought for the process of thinking. With reason as his god, he set about telling North Americans what to think, which is decidedly odd for someone who said he valued reason to the extent that he claimed. He held this position during a powerfully influential period that was driven by what's referred to as Mechanical Materialism, a belief that there's no such thing as a human soul and that the human body is a machine and nothing more.[14]

Freud also gave credence to the reason that's used as one is looking around and dismissed interest in looking up as a way to get clear about something.[15] Confidence in intuition (*nous*) got lost during modernity due to what we might call the idolatry of reason. As a result of his influence, Christians came to believe that, if they reflect on the motion (meaning-making) of their own souls, they're doing psychology not theology—a belief incongruent with Christian tradition (the first strand discussed earlier). And further, many came to think that, at best, their belief is infantile and often embarrassing. Freud was so influential in North American it's hard to persuade people of his influence on twentieth century atheism in the West (although he was not so influential in countries where Communism held sway).[16]

Healthy theological reflection includes *dianoia* and *nous*. Reason's cast of mind is as appropriate in theological reflection as anywhere else because conversation that moves to dialogue unites intuition (looking up) and reason (looking around). Theological reflection is informed by looking around at the world as a way to hold intuition accountable and by looking upward to receive insights from God that are informed by relying on the way that healthy reason operates in all its stubbornness to get clear about something. Yet in theological reflection, healthy reason is also humble and knows its appropriate place in its relationship with looking upward to gain spiritual insight.

As an example of the unity between looking up and looking around, in *Learning while Leading*, Anita Farber-Robinson explains a relationship between *dianoia* and *nous* (without using the terms) as they enhance human learning. Her book applies *Action Science* to theological reflection.[17] Her purpose is to improve the ability to look around at the world of objects, including oneself, as a way to become more effective in reflecting theologically. She wants to help people improve their effectiveness in ministry by inviting them to assess a central aspect of Action Science, i.e., directly observable data (looking around), and note their own responses to cues they get from the data they take on board from the world of objects, at the same time that they engage in self-observation. According to her model connecting spiritual insight and self-knowledge while assessing reality (directly observable data) is essential to personal learning.

In order to see how theological reflection can link *dianoia* and *nous*, let's explore further some modern assumptions about the role of reality in learning. At a theological conference, one presenter spoke on learning and made a claim that reality is unknowable. His is a commonly expressed view but it's misleading for a number of reasons.

If we say reality is unknowable, how could it be available in cues we use to evaluate and alter our understanding of what's going on? If reality were unknowable, how could we learn anything at all? Secondly, the claim is vague. Reality is multidimensional. As examples, I can know about someone. I know someone personally. I know what someone who's no longer alive thinks on a topic. I know a country I've never visited and can learn facts that those who live there don't know. I know what it's like to live in my own country in a way outsiders don't know.

I know the taste and smell of coffee. I know what an expression on someone's face signifies so I can respond appropriately. I know what someone is feeling by getting a sense of it while I'm in his or her presence, or by reading a book about his or her experience. I know what a teddy bear feels like and can make sense of what it means to a young child to have one to hold. I know about atoms but can't see them. I know God though I can't see God. I know some of these things because I experience their effects, just as I can't see the wind but can see its effects on the trees in my backyard.

To say reality is unknowable without distinguishing different ways we know something is misleading because it limits reality to its most complex, ineffable form. If we couldn't know real objects, we couldn't make sense of the world. The knowledge that infants acquire as they explore the world forms a basis for making the world meaningful so they can be sane. In terms of making the world meaningful, people continuously encounter objects, including people, and make sense of them. The terms objective and subjective have roots in this early experience. A subject, an infant, learns about objects by tasting, touching, smelling, hearing and seeing: subjectivity is constructed from experiencing the world in these ways. During the same period of infancy and toddlerhood, the young come to know that objects which can't be experienced directly at a given moment in time continue to exist outside the range of their senses, i.e., objects they can't see, hear, smell, touch or taste.[18]

What distances the subjective from the objective is the multi-dimensional nature of reality. Each object has more to it than a subject perceives. Some objects (atoms, God) can't be seen or assessed the way we experience teddy bears in a nursery. In addition, knowing is partial. While we say we can know what an expression on someone's face signifies, we also acknowledge that the data are only a beginning point, a theory. We need to ask the other some questions in order to check out our perception. When we believe we know something, it doesn't mean there's nothing more to know.

Let's consider the connection between 'knowing something' and 'making sense of something'. Knowing has to do with a capacity to make sense of the world by knowing enough about it to develop trust. Otherwise, as mentioned, people aren't sane. To say reality is unknowable is to make a vague statement that fails to distinguish partial from complete knowledge. To say I know God or atoms isn't to say I know everything about them, any more than to say I know my husband is to say I know everything about him.

This philosophical point resonates with scripture. In Ecclesiastes 3:11b we read that God "set eternity in the human heart; yet people cannot fathom what God has done from beginning to end." In I Corinthians 13:12 we read, "Now we see but a poor reflection as in a mirror; then we shall see face to face. Now I know in part; then I shall know fully, even as I am fully known." Reality is multi-dimensional; knowledge is partial. As a consequence, there's a relationship between *dianoia* and *nous*, i.e., looking around at the world, directly observable data, and looking up (receiving flashes of insight) that together inform theological reflection.

Another aspect of the second strand in reason's trajectory, which was present during the twentieth century West, was the exclusion of *nous* from the way reason was conceived. That problem takes us back to Kant and what he meant by privileging *Vernunft* (reason) over *Verstand* (intuition, intellection). As mentioned, people who came after him were happy to deify speculative reason. Kant foresaw this move and addressed it directly.

Reason could never be a god in Kant's system. In an essay he wrote towards the end of the 1700s, he analyzed the moment in which he found himself and considered the nature of reason. The essay is titled "What does it mean to orient oneself in thinking?" In it, he proposed that reason must have an orienting starting point. He argued for freedom to think that was unconstrained by political or religious authorities, but didn't argue for unlimited freedom to think *per se*. To him, freedom to think had to be grounded on something. That orienting point is reason's need for the existence of an Unlimited Being that is "original and all other beings [are] derived" from it. This is the orienting point for reason—a "a first *original being* as a supreme intelligence and at the same time as the highest good."[19] It was the existence of this original being that allowed reason its freedom—freedom from external supervision, but not freedom to go wherever it felt like going. Kant anticipated the twentieth century's adolescent impulse to believe that reason, if cut loose from political and religious authorities, would then have no limitations whatsoever.

Kant's point about reason's need for orientation was elaborated in the book, *On Certainty*, in which Wittgenstein asserted that all thought is grounded on assumptions we get through experience. Wittgenstein noted that people couldn't think at all without holding some basic assumptions, any more than we could go through a doorway if the door didn't have the very hinges that allow it to swing open.[20]

At the end of the 1700s, Kant described reason's orienting role in what he called its own needs. In addition to his certainty expressed in the maxim that, "it is necessary to orient oneself in the speculative use of reason"[21] (*speculatio*—attention to ultimate concerns), he identified two essential needs that reason has, which form around its need for an Original Being, i.e., God. These two needs were reason's dependence on the existence of Supreme Intelligence in order to have Intelligibility itself, and on a Being that is the Highest Independent Good in order to have any idea of what is good. There's also the implication in his essay that without the constraints of reason's own needs, the social and personal duties implied in reason also come unmoored. Kant expressed amazement at people who might in the future claim to use reason, yet also claim to be atheists.

In that essay, he argues that healthy reason relies on the existence of a Supreme Intelligent and Good Being. It couldn't simply take flight in whatever direction it might find appealing. The idea that unmoored freedom to think could do that—take flight in whatever direction it found attractive—was nonsense to him. Yet modern thinkers in the 1800s and 1900s held precisely that view. If someone believes that the freedom to think is limitless, it's easy to believe that thinking Christianly is a grave error that hobbles a person's capacity to use reason. But Christians shouldn't be misled by that modern mistake.

A point made earlier in this chapter conveys the difficulty Freud had with giving reason its unfettered freedom. He finally chose to tell people what to think, i.e., that they should think God doesn't exist. He chose reason as his god but insisted that there was only one proper move that reason could make: reason must produce unbelief. In so saying, he violated the very way reason has operated throughout the history of Western civilization—as that cast of mind, that stubborn effort to get clear about something that matters.

## SOULFUL THINKING

For those who wish to keep theological reflection alive to looking around as well as looking up, the trajectory of reason is instructive. Christianity holds other treasures too that help to refine, understand and use healthy reason, as one example, from its Latin tradition. In that tradition, reason has a similar division to the two Greek terms described earlier, and were terms that added value as they were used in Christian contexts.

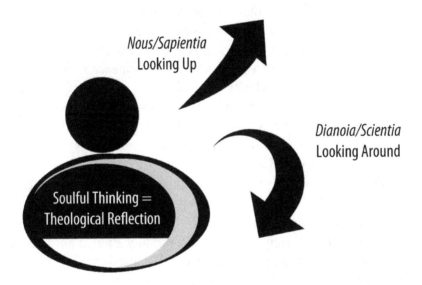

Latin terms for the Greek notions of *dianoia* and *nous*[22] were expanded in the terms *scientia* and *sapientia*. Ellen Charry explores the concept of *sapientia*, which like *nous*, refers to "engaged knowledge that connects the knower to the known,"[23] but was also a form of knowing that came to assume a need for trust in the object of its attention or awareness. *Sapience* "affects a knower positively and aids in his or her well-being."[24] She defines the term as having three characteristics: knowledge is assumed, reason is employed and trust is essential.[25] The Latin term *scientia* (like *dianoia*) is factual knowledge on which one makes rational judgments while *sapience* refers to discernment and thinking that leads to wisdom. To Augustine, *scientia* was preparation for *sapience*[26] so that two ways of knowing worked together in making sound judgments.[27] But *sapience* is a deeper and rich concept that implied a capacity for healing those who brought it into theological reflection.

As with *nous*, *sapientia* implies a connection to something larger than the person who seeks to be discerning, and comes "through insight, reflection, discernment, and inspiration as a result of thinking and guidance from a higher source."[28] It's fair to say that whenever we stand back and theorize, we engage with something larger than ourselves, e.g., wisdom based on accumulated human experience condensed into transferable knowledge or insight. Theological reflection relies on and results in wisdom. Yet the depth and richness of *sapience* is felt in the opportunity it offers to cleanse time for the purpose of knowing God; as believers spend time with God, they come to know more fully what they know about God. Theological reflection that incorporates *sapientia* relies on more than human wisdom; it's a sacred encounter with God.

Judeo-Christian traditions tend to use the word holy, *hagios* (αγιος), to apply to God and sacred, *hieros* (ιερος), to apply to things that are consecrated through the worship of God. In this chapter, sacred and holy are used interchangeably to emphasize some aspects of theological reflection that modernity seems to have forgotten, in particular, distinctions between sacred and profane uses of time. From a sacred perspective, a profane thing is deficient, broken, lost; it's common, vulgar, unworthy and isn't consecrated for any great purpose because it is or has become contaminated. Within a sacred worldview, a thing that's not usually profane can become so due to its condition of loss, by being disconnected from the sacred reality that holds together all things in a cosmos, since a cosmos is a living and articulated unity.[29] Sacred time becomes profane through misuse but there's always a cure provided by rituals of cleansing.[30]

*Sapientia* then, is a way of knowing that includes a sense of purification. It brings healing as an aspect of theological reflection, allowing Christians to unite reason and intuition, and therefore, to connect reason and faith. *Sapientia*, part of a sacred encounter with the Living God, permits believers to enjoy the benefits of God's presence and opens up access to wisdom from above (James 3:17).

From a sacred point of view, misusing time can't be erased or altered, but people can begin anew. *Sapience* has within itself, due to coming into the presence of a Holy God, the power to renew and refresh those who enter into theological reflection. Healing is experienced during time spent with God.

Scripture offers us the story of the prodigal as an example of what became profane through its disconnection from the Holy. Theological reflection—on one's own, with a witness, or in a group—permits people to come to their senses, reunite with God and be renewed. It's like returning home. If *sapience* is part of the process of theological reflection, trust is built in and is its outcome. Behind the possibility of theological reflection, is a patient, loving Father who awaits us, doesn't humiliate or punish, but celebrates our return. The separation itself is the punishment. The next chapter examines the stories of Cain and the Prodigal Son to contrast two examples about the role of *sapience* and healthy reason in theological reflection.

# Notes

1. Anthony Gottlier, *The Dream of Reason* (New York: W.W. Norton & Company, 216), xi.

2. Matthew 12:24-29

3. Joyce E. Bellous, *Educating Faith* (Edmonton, AB: Tall Pine Press, 2015), 1-76.

4. The focusing exercise is adapted from Eugene T. Gendlin's two books, *Experiencing and the Creation of Meaning* (New York: The Free Press of Glencoe, 1962) and also *Focusing* (New York: Bantam Books, second edition, 1981).

5. H. Smith, *The Soul of Christianity* (New York: Harper San Francisco, 2005), 27.

6. *Focusing,* 32.

7. *Focusing,* 118-122.

8. While Kant purified reason of its pre-modern misdirections, he also admitted its inherent limitations. See "What does it mean to orient oneself in thinking," in *Religion within the Boundaries of Mere Reason,* Allan Wood (Ed.), (Cambridge: Cambridge University Press, 1998), 3-14.

9. H. Caygill, *A Kant Dictionary,* (Oxford, UK: Blackwell, 1995).

10. F.E. Peters, *Greek Philosophical Terms,* (New York: New York University Press, 1967), 127.

11. *Greek Philosophical Terms,* 133.

12. *Greek Philosophical Terms,* 127.

13. *The Dream of Reason,* x.

14. *Educating Faith,* 191 -230.

15. Ana-Maria Rizzotu, *Why did Freud Reject God?*

16. Richard Dawkins, as one example, appears to believe he continues Freud's legacy as a prominent atheist.

17. Action Science is the product of work by two theorists Donald Schon and Chris Argyris. See the analysis of this practice in Anita Farber Robinson, *Learning While Leading* (An Alban Institute Publication, 2000), 40-56.

18. *Educating Faith,* 236.

19. Kant, *Religion within the Boundaries of Mere Reason,* (Allen Wood and George di Giovanni, Eds), What does it mean to orient oneself in thinking? (Cambridge: Cambridge University Press, 1998), 7.

20. *Educating Faith,* 236.

21. *Religion Within the Boundaries,* 3.

22. I do not suggest that this analysis of *dianoia* and *nous* captures everything that these terms imply.

23. E. Charry, *By the Renewing of Your Minds* (New York: Oxford University Press, 1997), 4.

24. *Renewing of Your Minds,* 7.

25. *Renewing of Your Minds,* 8.

26. *Renewing of Your Minds,* 237.

27. *Renewing of Your Minds,* 133.

28. *Renewing of Your Minds,* 133.

29. M. Eliade, *The Sacred and the Profane* (New York: Harcourt, Brace & World, Inc., 1959), 94.

30. In religious experience, time is not even—some is sacred, some is profane, i.e., ordinary temporal evanescent duration, not marked by depth and cycle as is sacred time, which remains constant, neither changed nor exhausted. In particular, sacred time reintegrates and renews so it has a therapeutic function. For non-religious people, time is linked to their own birth and death. Sacred time is non-historical and does not belong to the present only. It's in the present, does not change it, but adds to its significance: it's past, future and present — simultaneously. Christianity is also grounded on the historical reality that God was incarnated in the humanity of Jesus of Nazareth. Jesus' actions 2000 years ago still function for us because he is in the present interceding for us now. (Hebrews 7:25)

# CHAPTER 3

## SPEAKING THE TRUTH IN LOVE

---

Theological reflection includes thinking based on looking around and looking upward. As proposed in Chapter Two, it's not mere psychologizing. It's reflection on the movement of one's own soul that entails giving full attention to what we're thinking about God, others and ourselves. As a disciplined practice, it permits us to think new thoughts as we consider the soul's movement and open up to the presence of God in Jesus Christ, through the powerful work of the Holy Spirit. Truth-telling is the heart of its discipline. In coming home, the prodigal son didn't minimize his sin. Nor did his father. Rather, the father forgave him.

Chapter Two also describes Focusing and Artful Listening and points to their relationship with theological reflection. This chapter unpacks that relationship by describing four movements in the prodigal son story: leaving home, being away, coming to our senses and returning home. The Eastern Orthodox practice of what that tradition called 'guarding the heart' elaborates on what may be involved in coming to our senses and returning home. The purpose of this chapter is to reveal aspects of what's required as we seek spiritual intimacy with God, other people and with ourselves through theological reflection.

Witnesses who walk alongside someone who reflects theologically on a destabilizing situation are like the citizen in a far country in the prodigal son story. He provided an environment for the son to come to his senses. That environment was constituted by what the citizen did and didn't do for the son.

He provided a safe place without offering a surfeit of resources that might tempt a young man to stay with the pigs. Theological reflection gives and refuses to give certain kinds of support so that those who think about and with God can come to their senses and return home. Reflecting theologically by using scripture deepens our understanding of leaving home, being away, coming to our senses and returning to a place we thought we knew, but that we now can see in a new way.

## LEAVING HOME (LUKE 15:11-31)

The prodigal son left his father's household. It was a move that seemed necessary to him so that he could live his own life—or in modernity's terms—be free to think for himself and let his thinking go wherever it felt like going. He packed his bags and walked down the road. The elder son also left, but emotionally not physically. Without leaving, there's no coming back. Although it's not a good strategy for a response to conflict in general, leaving is part of growing up. Theological reflection helps us realize we've left home and need to do something about it. It arises in response to a destabilizing event. We're off balance, which is the evidence that we're no longer at home with God.

Not feeling at home may arise when something unexpected happens or come about due to something we think or do. Scripture is honest about human sin and declares that everyone sins. It also points out that sin creates distance from God. Not feeling at home with God may also be due to the concepts we have for God, other people (especially other Christians) or ourselves that don't fit what's going on within or around us. Suppose we think God is generous, giving and unconditionally loving, a fairly popular belief even among people who don't attend church.[1] If events occur that disappoint us, dissonance between expectations and what actually happens may create a need to rethink God. Disappointment also opens up a possibility to see God more fully and let our understanding of God keep pace with the way God wants to be known. Consider a conversation, recorded in Genesis, between God and Cain that conveys Cain's sin and disappointment.

Now Abel kept flocks, and Cain worked the soil. In the course of time, Cain brought some of the fruits of the soil as an offering to the Lord. But Abel brought fat portions from some of the firstborn of his flock. The Lord looked with favour on Abel and his offering, but on Cain and his offering he did not look with favour. So Cain was very angry, and his face was downcast.

Then the Lord said to Cain, "Why are you angry? Why is your face downcast? If you do what is right, will you not be accepted? But if you do not do what is right, sin is crouching at your door; it desires to have you, but you must master it."

Now Cain said to his brother Abel, "Let's go out to the field." And while they were in the field, Cain attacked his brother Abel and killed him.

Then the Lord said to Cain, "Where is your brother Abel?" "I don't know," he replied. "Am I my brother's keeper?" The Lord said, "What have you done? Listen! Your brother's blood cries out to me from the ground. Now you are under a curse and driven from the ground, which opened its mouth to receive your brother's blood from your hand. When you work the ground, it will no longer yield its crops for you. You will be a restless wanderer on the earth."

Cain said to the Lord, "My punishment is more than I can bear. Today you are driving me from the land, and I will be hidden from your presence; I will be a restless wanderer on the earth, and whoever finds me will kill me." But the Lord said to him, "Not so; anyone who kills Cain will suffer vengeance seven times over." Then the Lord put a mark on Cain so that no one would kill him. So Cain went out from the Lord's presence and lived in the land of Nod, east of Eden. (Genesis 4:2-16)

---

**Reflective Questions**

What's going on in this passage? Right now, spend time and write out your reactions to the story. Please do this recording before you read any further. Be as explicit in what you think as you can.

### BEING AWAY

One way to reflect on the Cain story includes the following: The difference between the offerings given to the Lord may have been in the gift itself or in the attitude of giving it. Whatever its source, Cain knew intimacy with God. The Creator came to speak with him. God's act is remarkable. Their intimacy wasn't shut down by Cain's mistake. It shut down due to his refusal to master himself and make amends. He left God's presence not because of sin; he left because he chose to live in sin instead of seeking forgiveness. God was willing; Cain wasn't. He refused to do the hard work of being restored. God invited him to cooperate in his own recovery but the young man refused to reconsider what God required of him. He asked no questions. The prodigal son also left his household to find his own way elsewhere.

What do you notice in this passage? Do you see elements of your experience in Cain? How does your life story compare with Cain's story? Describe for yourself how God acted in this passage? What surprises you? What confuses you? What do you think God's tone of voice was as he spoke with Cain? Why do you think that? What's the range of possibility for God's tone of voice and facial expression as he meets with Cain? What does God want from Cain?

The prodigal son came to his senses in a pig field but still felt he must devalue himself to earn his way back to his father. The father paid no attention to the low view of self the son brought back home. Instead, he gave him a ring, a robe and threw a party to welcome him. If theological reflection is to be effective, the attitude we take toward others and ourselves must be based on the Father's friendly, loving response to his son's return.

What's God's tone of voice and facial expression when you realize you have done what's wrong and are in the wrong place? What is God doing as you sense you're far away, standing in a mess of sin, a mess that may be due to your sin or someone else's? What does it feel like to come to our senses? To become aware of the process, reflect on your response to Cain. Compare the conversation you imagined between God and Cain with an encounter recorded between God, Satan and the high priest Joshua. The Zechariah passage offers a glimpse of God's feeling for us and helps us hear how God speaks. Read the passage carefully a few times. As you read it, at some point, substitute your own for Joshua's name.

> Then he showed me Joshua the high priest standing before the angel of the Lord, and Satan standing at his right side to accuse him. The Lord said to Satan, "The Lord rebuke you, Satan! The Lord who has chosen Jerusalem, rebuke you! Is not this man a burning stick snatched from the fire?"
>
> Now Joshua was dressed in filthy clothes as he stood before the angel. The angel said to those who were standing before him, "Take off his filthy clothes." Then he said to Joshua, "See, I have taken away your sin, and I will put rich garments on you." Then I said, "Put a clean turban on his head." So they put a clean turban on his head and clothed him, while the angel of the Lord stood by.
>
> The angel of the Lord gave this charge to Joshua: "This is what the Lord Almighty says: 'If you walk in my ways and keep my requirements, then you will govern my house and have charge of my courts, and I will give you a place among these standing here.'" (Zech. 3:1-7)

---

**Reflective Questions**

What's going on in this passage? Right now, spend time and write out your reactions to the story. Please do this recording before you read any further. Be as explicit in what you think as you can.

---

The following are some issues raised by the passage and its application to theological reflection: What did the Lord say to Satan? The passage is worth meditating on. Its pattern echoes central dynamics in Focusing, Eastern Orthodox practice and Freud's insight about recovery through psychoanalysis (although Freud didn't use religious language or imagery and neither does Gendlin).

Joshua came to his senses by realizing God was speaking on his behalf. Satan accused him, not God. If theological reflection is effective, its environment assures us that God is friendly. God's friendliness grounds the compassion we extend to ourselves and to others. Notice that Joshua's garments were removed. He was exposed long enough to receive new garments—an act that took place in a safe environment. If there's any emotional exposure during theological reflection, it's for the purpose of self-observation, remembering that God advocates for us. It's brief, uncomfortable, but not an end in itself. It's not something we're trying to make happen; it's simply part of healing.

In summary, an important step in theological reflection is realizing we no longer feel at home with God or with someone who's important to us. If we sense that distance, it's because something is wrong. That realization comes through observing our feelings and thoughts about our present situation. We might realize we're angry, worried, scared, lonely or hungry for God and/or for healthy relationships with other people.

### COMING TO OUR SENSES

Cain and Joshua give insight into patterns of thinking and speaking that either keep us on a pig farm or lead us home. To return home, we must first come to our senses. Coming to our senses has two dimensions: we realize where we are; we realize where we want to end up. Taken together, Cain and Joshua convey essential elements of God's attitude toward us and his expectations for us.

God humanized Cain by summoning him to master himself. He spoke to Cain's humanity and symbolically established the humanity in all of us. God sustained Joshua's humanity despite the sin that's symbolized by his filthy clothes. Actions of God humanize while actions of Satan dehumanize people. Unfortunately, we sometimes participate in that dehumanization. The prodigal son's self-deprecation is an example. He engages unhealthy reason. As the father in the parable makes clear, God isn't interested in making us feel guilty or devaluating us. It's only Satan that loves to trash our humanity.

There are other scriptural examples that summon and sustain

humanity, for example, themes of loss and recovery in Ezekiel and Hosea. The perfect example of summoning and sustaining our humanity is found in the death and resurrection of Jesus Christ. To return home to God is to become more human, to love humanity itself. Our restored humanity is the impetus to discover significant themes that present themselves in theological reflection. But the difference between Cain and the prodigal son stands out. God invites us to come home but doesn't command it. Freedom is part of the human condition and God doesn't diminish that humanity through force.

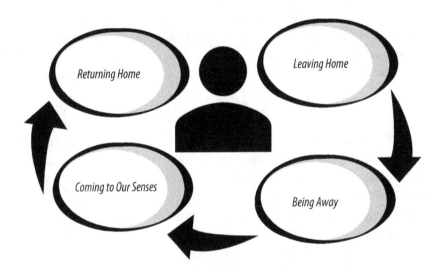

As mentioned, the prodigal son story includes a citizen in the far country where the son finally found himself. During collaborative theological reflection, outlined in chapter one, other people act as citizens in a far country and create an environment in which it's possible to speak the truth in love (in a loving environment) as a way to summon and sustain the humanity of the one who struggles. In theological reflection, the truth can be told. If citizens (witnesses) offer help, they refuse to use unhealthy reason. There's remarkable congruence between secular and scriptural descriptions of unhealthy reason. We shouldn't be surprised. All truth is God's truth. God invests in our humanity as we turn for help and tell the truth, even from the middle of a pig field.

---

**Reflective Questions**

Consider how you speak about yourself or other people that, in the past, has led you to renewal. How is that pattern of thinking and acting different from ones that keep you locked in sin? Write out some of each type of pattern. Is there any new insight that emerges as you write them down? Are there insights in each pattern that you are very frustrated with but that you continue to notice in yourself? Does the concept of *sapience* (in chapter two) suggest anything to you about your own recovery? If it's helpful, re-read Joshua's story and considers his recovery. Like Joshua, give your fullest attention to God's voice as one that welcomes, affirms and strengthens your resolve to come to your senses.

---

## FREUD, SELF-OBSERVATION AND SPIRITUAL HEALTH

The Focusing exercise outlined earlier depends for its effectiveness on learning to silence the voice that belittles the significance of a problem that's destabilizing us, or may even have been traumatic. In order to have courage to listen to our hearts and speak the truth, we need a supportive environment. To heal hurts inherent in our troubles, that environment will be infused with God's presence and grace.

Christian life promises God's presence. Jesus said "surely I am with you always, to the very end of the age." (Matthew 28:20) Maturity in Christ and friendship with God are core benefits of believing in Jesus. Church communities can be poor in faith, especially due to Western Christianity's position in the aftermath of modern prejudices against faith and belief in God, as described in the previous chapter. Yet a democratic urge in Christianity invites us to believe we can all be close to God. Self-observation and spiritual healing are two Christian practices that facilitate a safe place for those who long to know God and themselves more fully. To provide for that healing, given the trust that's implicit in *sapience*, we must learn how to silence the ways of speaking to ourselves and other people that tend to prevent our growth in God's grace.

There are Christian and secular voices that seem to agree on how to become adept at self-observation. In addition to Focusing, Freud's perspective on the work clients must do to observe themselves also permits healing to take place. His insights echo another Christian tradition that affirms essential aspects of self-observation. That tradition is found in Eastern Orthodoxy.

As mentioned, self-observation is at the heart of theological reflection. A capacity to observe the movement of our own souls and invite God to inform and transform the spiritual meaning we're in the midst of making is central to becoming a mature believer. Yet during the modern period, in many ways, Freud took over Christian practices and removed their spiritual quality. While he was simply incorrect in some of his theories, in particular to position sexuality as the dominant cause of anxiety,[2] he retained an emphasis on self-observation that's not only congruent with pre-modern Christian practices but is instructive for how healing through self-observation actually might work.

During analysis of a destabilizing situation, in Freud's terms, we observe ourselves effectively if we silence the skeptic. The ego (his term for a personality's organizing system) systematizes or organizes experience and works toward a healthy engagement with reality. The ego's work is complicated by the id (everything inherited at birth) and superego (a precipitate of parental influence as far as Freud was concerned that could function as Satan did with Joshua).[3] As the ego organizes experience, some misdirection can occur: a train of thought can run off its rails. Suppose the ego experiences trauma—an event that makes too many demands on the personality. The ego misdirects itself if it tries to solve its internal problem and address trauma by interpreting its own suffering and telling a narrative about what to expect from the world based on its unavoidable use of unhealthy reason.

Freud's solution to ego misdirection (psychoanalysis)

replaced spiritual healing in the twentieth century western society. He stopped speaking of souls and started talking about psyches. But if we closely examine what he proposed, his descriptions resemble pre-modern Christian beliefs and practices about how to be spiritually well. The point of contact between Freud and Eastern Orthodox tradition is a practice of self-observation. Freud believed that if a troublesome idea could be traced back to elements in the patient's past, it simultaneously crumbled away and the patient was free from it. Christians believe we must bring the idea to God and surrender it to him, with help from the Holy Spirit and Christ's example. Yet Freud's perspective is useful to see how surrender might work. His prescription for health was: Tell me everything.[4]

He saw that in order for patients to get well they must learn to observe their own thinking. In self-observation, patients prepare by paying full attention to their own psyche (soul) and by eliminating criticism that normally drifted through those thoughts, such as those listed in the Focusing exercise described in the last chapter. Resting on a couch with eyes closed was pre-requisite for the concentration needed to give full attention to self-observation.

From a Christian perspective, the environment we create for theological reflection will convey that God is Friendly. Given that friendly environment, the following example from Freud's work is so useful it's worth quoting in full. Freud observed that if a particular man is trying to observe himself, a psychiatrist first insists that he renounce all criticism of his thought, as it is being perceived:

> We therefore tell him that the success of the psychoanalysis depends upon his noticing and reporting whatever comes into his head and not being misled, for instance, into suppressing an idea because it seems to him meaningless. He must adopt a completely impartial attitude to what occurs to him, since it is precisely his critical attitude, which is responsible for his being unable, in the ordinary course of things, to achieve the desired unraveling of his dream or [obsessive] idea or whatever it may be. I have noticed in my psychological work that the whole frame of mind of a man who is

reflecting is totally different from that of a man who is observing his own psychical [soulful] processes.[5]

Freud saw that self-observation had a very different quality to reflection that was caught up in what was described earlier as unhealthy reason. He noted that

> In reflection, there is one more psychical activity at work than in the most attentive self-observation, and this is shown amongst other things by the tense looks and wrinkled forehead of a person pursuing his reflections as compared with the restful expression of the self-observer. In both cases, attention must be concentrated, but the man who is reflecting is also exercising his critical faculty; this leads him to reject some of the ideas that occur to him after perceiving them, to cut short others without following the train of thought which they would open up for him, and to behave in such a way towards others that they never become conscious at all and are accordingly suppressed before being perceived.[6]

In these words, Freud pointed out the necessity to suspend some of the ways we think. To him, the skeptical voice is a critical faculty that uses unhealthy reason. If unhealthy reason is silenced, someone trying to observe what they carry in their own heart can pay full attention to the meaning that drives the way they make sense of the world.

What a particular self-observer is trying to get at is the current meaning she's making of her experience. It's not about being right. It's about hearing the story she's telling herself about what an event means. Self-observation allows her to get at that meaning if she suspends unhealthy reason. As Freud put it:

> The self-observer on the other hand need only take the trouble to suppress his critical faculty. If he succeeds in doing that, innumerable ideas come into his consciousness of which he could otherwise never have got hold. The material, which is in this way freshly obtained for his self-perception, makes it possible to interpret both his pathological ideas and his dream-structures.[7]

In theological reflection, we're concerned with ordinary human (existential) experience. Self-observation gives attention to following the path of our own thought, and like Freud, health isn't produced by censuring thought but by allowing someone to interpret it. In theological reflection, we have access to healthy reason as we suspend unhealthy reason. As we speak the truth in love, with a witness who knows how to listen, healing emerges along with insight from God to re-organize the story we're telling that has destabilized us.

Consider the images of Cain and Joshua. For both, God had an interpretation of what was going on that wasn't available to either of them. The stories Cain and Joshua were telling themselves appear to keep them trapped. The best narrative that the prodigal son could imagine was to convince himself to be a servant not a son in his father's household. He couldn't imagine forgiveness and restoration.

For Freud, the aim of self-observation was to offer a talking cure that relied on human intervention, as if the psychoanalyst must do the work of healthy reason that clients couldn't accomplish by themselves. He was clear that if unhealthy reason is deployed at the wrong time, in the wrong way, it forecloses on healthy insights that might emerge.

In theological reflection, people in distress are invited to hear scripture in order to find new narratives to refine the one they currently tell themselves. To find renewal, they first need to hear the story they're telling themselves in the present moment. Many believers tell a story about God they got from experience, not from scripture. These stories include ways of describing the human condition that are less than human and certainly not humane. They tell the God Story in ways that are neither friendly nor liberating.

Theological reflection, at its best, allows our stories to be heard and refreshed by the truth of scripture, which reveals the character of God. The Bible describes God's love and persistence that allow us to return to his loving embrace. Yet the tendency to use unhealthy reason is powerful and pervasive in human history. Let's look again to Christian traditions that have other ways to talk back to its evil effects.

## RETURNING HOME BY GUARDING THE HEART

In the history of Eastern Orthodoxy, unhealthy reason's evil effects were challenged by a practice called Guarding the Heart. In that Niptic tradition, as monks gained experience as followers of Jesus, they learned to suspend certain ways of thinking due to their perception of the disturbance these thoughts created in their inmost being. The practice was learned in the presence of monks who had mastered themselves, as God invited Cain to do.

To begin with, as an inexperienced monk tried to perceive what was really on his heart, (only men could be monks) his heart made use of reason after self-observation had done its work. In this tradition, reason was not a stand-alone. Monks understood that reason needs material to work upon. Its function is to draw conclusions and form concepts from data provided by revelation, spiritual knowledge and sense-observation.

In Eastern Orthodoxy, knowledge produced by healthy reason was a lower form than spiritual knowledge since it didn't imply direct apprehension or perception of divine truth. For them, *nous* was an activity of the intellect. Spiritual knowledge, *gnosis* (γνωσις), was different from knowledge that came through human reason.[8] *Nous* was inspired by God and linked to contemplation. Intuiting was greater than reasoning because it was a form of receiving insight from God, while even healthy reason involved a human agent much more fully in its construction. Knowledge that didn't come directly from God had less value because it more clearly involved fallen human beings. They distinguished healthy from unhealthy reason by appealing to the doctrine of the Fall, recorded in Genesis.

This tradition held the view that, to remain healthy, acquiring knowledge from God was grounded on careful, continuous reading of scripture and required the faithful to immerse themselves in corporate worship with followers of Jesus. The spiritual work of someone receiving knowledge from God was to be an open, clean receiver. A capacity to be open and clean developed through the discipline of becoming an experienced monk in the company of the faithful, through worshipping God and knowing scripture.

In the growth of Christian maturity, using early Eastern Orthodox practices, there was a crucial difference between experienced and inexperienced monks. Inexperienced monks had to learn how to catch thoughts (temptations) as they entered consciousness. They learned to observe each thought and attend to it. As thought entered, it was identified. They told themselves to stop thinking evil thoughts. They believed they could stop thought and be effective in doing so, with help from the Holy Spirit. They practised arguing with their own thinking—a process they called rebuttal, like a lawyer arguing in court.

The task of rebuttal was to recognize, counter, expose and destroy evil thoughts. In this context, evil impressions were thought to infiltrate the intellect in the image of material things. The Jesus prayer (Lord Jesus Christ, Son of God, have mercy on me) was used to rebut evil thought since monks knew that an activity of God's grace was effective in destroying evil, not human striving. The monk strove to be attentive; victory belonged to God. He aspired to a certain kind of life that meant being a friend of God—one who lived fully Christ's invitation to eternal life. [The gender exclusive pronouns used throughout this section reflect historical accuracy. There's no intention here to suggest that only men can achieved this quality of spiritual maturity.][9]

As one example of temptation and struggle, St Isaiah the Solitary, a fourth or fifth century Desert Father, reflected the spirituality of Egypt and Palestine to portray a poignant battle in an inexperienced monk. He wrote that

> So long as the contest continues, a man is full of fear and trembling, wondering whether he will win today or be defeated, whether he will win tomorrow or be defeated: the struggle and stress constrict his heart. But when he has attained dispassion, the contest comes to an end; he receives the prize of victory and has no further anxiety about the three that were divided, for now through God they have made peace with one another. These three are the soul, the body and the spirit. When they become one through the energy of the

Holy Spirit, they cannot again be separated. Do not think, then, that you have died to sin, so long as you suffer violence, whether waking or sleeping, at the hands of your opponents....While a man is still competing in the arena, he cannot be sure of victory.[10]

The spiritual struggle of the faithful is to achieve unity of heart: willing, thinking, feeling and doing. Dispassion, to St Isaiah, didn't imply that passion is negative. Dispassion is purity of heart—a state of reintegration and spiritual freedom.

The spiritual work of an inexperienced monk was to be attentive so he could overcome the enemy of the soul's joy, the demons. Recall that in the Zechariah passage, Satan is active. Monks were determined to see in opposition to spiritual growth the effort of one enemy only. Satan alone was blamed for spiritual strife. They were to attend to their own sins and practice repentance rather than dwelling on the sins of others. They didn't blame others for their suffering and inner struggle but held themselves accountable. As scripture says, our struggle is not against flesh and blood. To these monks, demons had as their unremitting purpose to prevent the heart from being attentive because they knew that its attentiveness enriches a human soul with such spiritual liveliness that they worked hard against its fulfillment. As monks gain wisdom through spiritual effort, with help from wisdom from above (James 3:17) they acquire insight into the behavior of other believers.

The process of inner spiritual work countered Satan's provocation through stopping a thought and/or arguing with it. Monks marked murderous, predatory thoughts as they approached the heart and paid attention to them. They described a pattern of sin's descent that expanded on James 1:12-15; 4:7-8a.

In that tradition, as an evil thought enters consciousness, provoked by demons, a monk's own thought chases after it and enters into impassioned engagement with it. When a monk was inexperienced, he tried to stop these thoughts at the soul's gate. He shunned evil thoughts in order to experience inner quietness that allowed him to converse with God. He practiced experiencing inner peace and its joys so he had good reasons for returning to it if he sensed that some thought, word or action disquieted this inner sanctuary. The pattern of temptation was outlined as follows: Provocation, engagement, agreement, action and the sin itself.[11] Sin was characterized as a form of captivity in which engagement with evil thoughts grew habitual, continuous and became relentless passion aimed at attaining the thing desired. In sin itself, passion was negative and depicted as captivity.

To demonstrate the process, suppose someone humiliates a monk. Immediately he thinks of revenge. He's provoked. The thought presents itself unbidden. He considers revenge. The thought of revenge enters consciousness. Yet in provocation, a thought is still free from passion if the image entering the heart is glimpsed by the intellect. A monk might realize that he's thinking about getting revenge. All is lost if he doesn't realize he wants revenge because he'll simply act out of that desire and fail to be self-observant.

If he observes the thought, he has an opportunity to consider revenge fully. If a monk engages the thought, he converses with it in an impassioned or a dispassionate way. He considers revenge and pictures the action of humiliating the one who injured him. At this point he has several options. If he gives assent, he accords with the thought and focuses on the pleasure of revenging himself. He imagines the other's discomfort and that image gives him pleasure. At this point, he may act subtly to seek revenge through gossip or by trying to gain support from other monks to help him fulfil his desire for revenge. Of course, he may instead seek support from others to help him undermine the desire itself.

If he becomes captive to a desire for revenge, the image of humiliating another fills his mind—nothing else matters—he thinks of little else. If he takes action, he has moved toward the sin itself. In the sin itself, captivity is all encompassing; it becomes a persistent engagement with an image of humiliating the other and disrupts his inner quiet. When passion is negative, it lurks in the soul over a long period as a hoarded desire in the heart. But a monk isn't guilty for considering revenge due to the feeling that springs upon him when he feels humiliated; he's guilty if he takes action and marries the desire.

Regarding the first three stages of temptation, provocation is sinless, engagement isn't entirely free of sin; action is dangerous and sinfulness as assent or agreement depends upon the inner state of the monk. In an experienced monk, something is different. He recognizes temptation. He isn't a novice. He may see that in a particular case, revenge is clearly justified. But even if justified, he has other things to consider. If he chooses to act because his action arises from captivity to the thought desired, his inner life is controlled by that desire and he is therefore not free in Christ, but is captive to sin.

It's important to mark the stages to see how healthy reason operates in a monk's life. Over time, he learns to identify reasons for taking or refusing to take revenge. If he's humiliated, he brings healthy reason to bear on his feeling. In doing so, he refuses to engage with unhealthy reason that tempts him to belittle himself or drown in humiliation. This is a hopeful view of temptation. Both repentance and punishment educate the monk by giving him an arsenal of his true and best reasons when temptation beckons to him again. It's a mistake to think he's wrong to consider revenge if humiliated.

By reflecting on revenge, he offers himself reasons acquired through experience and considers the full outcome of seeking revenge. He sifts through what's involved in carrying it out and in refusing to do so. He slows down the process of thinking to remember his true and best reasons for being a follower of Jesus, of being God's beloved. There's no reason to think that the experienced monk will continue to permit someone to humiliate him, even if he refuses to engage revenge. He now has new insights about the other that can make him wise in his dealings with that person.

For him, reason isn't self-depreciation but takes account of the cost of revenge. Scripture is brought to bear on temptation. Reason offers insight into what happens if people carry out revenge. His action affirms scripture and strengthens his resolve to use reason to calculate costs in advance. He isn't captive to the desire to enact revenge. He acts reasonably.

But suppose he chooses to remain captive to the desire for revenge. His struggle at this point will bring punishment or victory—punishment because he's caught out, victory if he gets away with it. But in faith community, he must live with the consequences of either outcome. If he's victorious, he has now spread the harm of humiliation among his community. If he remains alive to self-observation, he recognizes in another the conditions of harm he felt in himself. In community, he can't escape the social cost of his sin.

If he sins, he has the option to repent and be renewed. His punishment can be the means by which he comes to his senses. If he does sin and pursues revenge, the compassion inherent in his community helps to acknowledge the costs incurred by everyone when one person sins. Perhaps this is why monks in this tradition thought the practice was dangerous unless carried out in community. For all of us, in spending time with God, we can be healed. Instructed by sin, we get good reasons for not succumbing to temptation. Moral formation strengthens theological reflection as it operates in this way. Healing offers hope.

The monk who stops the initial provocation, argues effectively with it or regards it dispassionately, and has at one stroke cut off the sinful stages that follow.[12] Becoming an experienced monk, on the other hand, requires him to admit these thoughts in order to learn to censure actions that arise from marrying them. We could say the experienced monk can't be fooled by the attraction of seeking revenge. He knows its havoc too well. It's not that he blindly obeys the rules. He weighs the full consequences of taking action, one of which is obedience[13] and decides how he wants to influence the world. Thoughts of revenge are always dangerous but they aren't necessarily fatal.

A monk experienced in spiritual warfare, recognizes and defuses the power of a false image of satisfaction secured by revenge and retains his inner quietness. He may still take action to rectify the wrong but does so without sinning. Experienced monks were clear that it's not only evil thoughts that lead astray. Good thoughts can lead to disaster, if taken to excess. They did battle with all thought. They allowed thoughts to enter and discerned those that were from the enemy—whether they appeared good or evil at first glance.

Is self-observation on this ancient model nothing more than a repression of thought? It's not. It's the self-regulation of thought. It comes through observing the movement of one's own soul. It results in freedom from being manipulated by one's own thought life[14] and the tyranny of temptation.

Further, there's a similarity between experienced monks and Freud's successful patients: reason must wait until we discern its health of its lack of it. For those unable to succeed at self-observation (Focusing), Freud proposed the following:

> The ground for your complaint seems to lie in the constraint imposed by your reason upon your imagination. It seems a bad thing and detrimental to the creative work of the mind if Reason makes too close an examination of the ideas as they come pouring in—at the very gateway, as it were. Looked at in isolation, a thought may seem very trivial or very fantastic; but it may be made important by another thought that comes after it, and, in conjunction with other thoughts that may seem equally absurd, it may turn out to form a most effective link.[15]

It seems as if the psychoanalyst takes the place of the monk's faith community in Freud's approach, although he doesn't consider the self-discipline that grows in the inexperienced monk as a possibility for his patients. His patients haven't been able to quiet their hearts.

Yet in both practices, reason has to wait. To regulate our thought life, we wait to perceive a felt sense of what's disturbing our inmost being. To Freud,

> Reason cannot form an opinion upon all of this unless it retains the thought long enough to look at it in connection with the others. On the other hand, where there is a creative mind, Reason—so it seems to me—relaxes its watch upon the gates, and the ideas rush

in pell-mell, and only then does it look them through and examine them in a mass....relaxation of the watch upon the gates of Reason, the adoption of an attitude of uncritical self-observation, is by no means difficult to achieve....[and] patients succeeded after their first instructions.[16]

When Freud talks about relaxing the watch upon the mind's gate, monks would say that we don't relax so much as pay attention to them, but the effects are the same in terms of making reason wait. If we see that Freud assumes gate watchers pour down unhealthy reason on thoughts as they struggle to reach the gate, the similarity is easier to see.

It's hard to find clear instructions given to Freud's patients, but Gendlin's instruction for Focusing seems congruent with his purposes. For monks and Freud's patients, reason had to be discerned and learned. Regulating thought life comes with the discipline implied in companionship with other people who understand and interpret experience with us. As with Joshua, self-depreciation and hopelessness are the voice of Satan, a voice we learn to identify and reject, as scripture says, "resist the devil and he will flee from you. Draw near to God and he will draw near to you." (James 4:8)

An experienced monk pursued obedience not because he feared getting caught at being vengeful. He was moved by love, wanting his inner life to house God, as scripture says, Christ in you the hope of glory. (Colossians 1:27b) He was motivated by friendship with God, as scripture says, "I no longer call you servants, because servants do not know their master's business. Instead, I have called you friends, for everything that I learned from my father I have made known to you." (John 15:15) These monks saw the possibility of friendship with God as a goal worth pursuing. Guarding the Heart from passion that would ruin the inner life was compellingly attractive. Likewise, an environment for theological reflection aims to create and encourage a desire to draw near to God in friendship. In the act of drawing near, there's still much to learn about God.

## RETURNING

The most remarkable realization occurred when the prodigal got back. He saw the farm in a new way. It had dimensions he never noticed before. He hadn't really understood his father. If we learn to govern our own souls by observing and guarding them, we have an opportunity to see God anew. This is the purpose of theological reflection:

> So he got up and went to his father. But while he was still a long way off, his father saw him and was filled with compassion for him; he ran to his son, threw his arms around him and kissed him. The son said to him, "Father, I have sinned against heaven and against you. I am no longer worthy to be called your son. But the father said to his servants, 'Quick! Bring the best robe and put it on him. Put a ring on his finger and sandals on his feet. Bring the fattened calf and kill it. Let's have a feast and celebrate. For this son of mine was dead and is alive again; he was lost and is found.' So they began to celebrate. (Luke 15:20-24)

The prodigal son learned what God is like through experience. Theological reflection is our opportunity to consider the way we act and think about God, others and ourselves and to observe the movement of our souls as we make meaning, because the growth of our human "consciousness is the foundation of things."[17]

Perhaps Focusing is what modern philosopher Hegel meant by self-conscious reflection on self-consciousness, i.e., the process of observing the flow of meaning being made in the soul. Maybe, if Gendlin got tapes of Hegel talking, he might have identified a similar process in the philosopher that he found in his own research. Hegel's work is the heart of educational processes that John Dewey and Paulo Freire developed to help people see the meaning they were making in the soul. Freire referred to the process as *conscientization*.

As they come home to God, Christians secure healing through the Holy Spirit. As the faithful learn to observe themselves and the meaning they've made and the meaning they're making, they engage in the spiritual work of theological reflection and can home to see God, scripture and experience in new ways. Coming home usually requires us to collaborate with other people.

Paulo Freire is a good way forward as we try to get a grasp of theological reflection and its use of healthy reason. Following his Hegelian approach, using self-conscious awareness of self-conscious experience, Freire taught literacy to villagers in South America. His theory and examples explain further what's involved in applying scripture to life in a way that encompasses the central gospel reality of Christ's death and resurrection. We're resurrection people who begin again, during theological reflection in the Presence of God and other people, to create a community that welcomes us home from the pig fields of ordinary living—if that's where we find ourselves.

# Notes

1.  Christian Smith refers to a view that he uncovered in his data in the book *Soul Searching* (New York: Oxford University Press, 2005), 162-163. The view is Moralistic Therapeutic Deism, which primarily depicts God as a Counselor in the Sky whose only interest in us is that we be happy.

2.  Jerome Kagan, *Galen's Prophecy* (Boulder, Colorado: Basic Books, 1998), 85.

3.  There's no intention to equate parental influence (or any person's influence) with Satan; that's not the point. But there is a similarity in the function of those internal 'voices' that accuse, blame and belittle and the role of Satan depicted in this scripture passage.

4.  Sigmund Freud, *The Interpretation of Dreams*, (London: Penguin Books, 1991), 174.

5.  *Interpretation of Dreams*, 176.

6.  *Interpretation of Dreams*, 176.

7.  *Interpretation of Dreams*, 176.

8.  Spiritual knowledge was misused in Gnosticism, which was an extreme

form of the practice that's at the core of guarding the heart. In guarding the heart, a monk is trying to listen to his own inmost being, his own soul, and isn't claiming to have special knowledge other than insight into his own needs, desires and motives.

9.  See for example, Brown's *The Body and Society* to find remarkable examples of the spiritual maturity and discipline of women in this historical period.

10. G.E.H. Palmer, et al. *The Philokalia, Vol. 1,* (London: Faber and Faber, 1979), 29.

11. *Philokalia, Vol. 1,* 171.

12. G.E.H. Palmer, et al. *The Philokalia, Vol. 3* (London: Faber and Faber, 1984), 29.

13. Dorothee Solle, *Creative Disobedience* (Cleveland, Ohio: The Pilgrim Press, 1995).

14. Alexander Nehamas, *The Art of Living* (Berkeley, CA: The University of California Press, 1998), 179.

15. *The Interpretation of Dreams,* 177-178.

16. *The Interpretation of Dreams,* 177-178.

17. *Soul of Christianity,* 117.

# PART II

# PERSONAL THEOLOGICAL REFLECTION

CHAPTER 4

# GENERATIVE THEMES AND PERSONAL INQUIRY

nvesting in healthy theological reflection makes us more
human as well as more faithful. With Cain and Joshua, God
instilled and supported their humanity and symbolically did
so for all of us. Theological reflection is a humanizing process
with Jesus' humanity at its core. Like Jesus, we reject Satan's voice
as well as reasoning that belittles or diminishes our humanity.
Reflecting theologically also moves us to find big pictures for
understanding what's going on in a destabilizing event so we can
situate it in wider frameworks of culture, scripture, community
and personal inquiry. As we situate our own difficulties in a
broader context, we're better able to connect what's disturbing
us with what scripture teaches us.

That bigger picture is layered with significant themes that
South American educator Freire called generative themes. A
generative theme is formed from observing elements within the
destabilizing event itself. These themes reveal aspects of spiritual
work we need to do in order to come to our senses and return
home. This chapter explores Freire's notion of generative themes
and applies the idea to two case studies. The case studies and the
reflection that goes along with them act as models for how to
reflect on ordinary human experience in ministry contexts. The
purpose of the chapter is to show how we can get the most from
scripture as we reflect on what's disturbing us.

As an example, there are central, humanizing themes in Cain's
story. Cain had a presenting problem he couldn't understand.

His sacrifice wasn't accepted. Instead of talking to God or his brother, he seethed in anger and ultimately chose to solve his dilemma by himself. One major generative theme in his story is isolation. Even though his people were right there, he felt isolated and operated out of that isolation. God came close to him but he refused to consider God's offer of insight: 'Sin is crouching at your door, but you must master it'. He chose to kill Abel rather than communicate with him.

Recall the first interpretation God made of humanity: "it's not good for the man to be alone" (Genesis 2:18). We tend to think of this statement as instructive of marriage but it also applies to Cain. He longed to be in God's Presence—without leaving room for his brother. He wanted relationship, yet solved his problems alone. He asked no questions. In isolation, resentment took over. He came to think that thoughts circulating inside his own head were the truth, the only truth. And these 'truths' led him to think he had only one option.

Like an inexperienced monk who fails to stop evil thought at the soul's gate, he plotted revenge and carried it out. He shows us what happens if we let isolation prevent communion with God and other people. There are other generative themes as well. Once he killed Abel, Cain feared other people. There are family dynamics we can only surmise since we aren't given more details, which is why the story functions so well for us as we bring our own expectations and experiences to it.

A generative theme is humanizing if it lets us see in what ways we're like and unlike Cain. He was caught inside his view of God. He had options. God offered help for the isolation that didn't end when he murdered his brother—the murder solved nothing. God put a sign of protection on him as he sent him out of his immediate, intimate Presence. God saw that he feared other people and responded to alleviate that fear. Cain's story shows that generative themes contain contradictions, which, if unpacked and understood, reveal a way forward towards reconciliation. Cain wanted to be in God's Presence and be accepted; he wanted to annihilate his brother's freedom to be in God's Presence when Abel's sacrifice was accepted.

Cain shows us what human beings are like and demonstrates how not to act, but his story also reveals what God is like. He could have listened to God. Cain acknowledged a desire for God's Presence that didn't diminish even though he sinned. God initiated a move toward Cain after the murder; this is astonishing. He and God were still in relationship. It was Cain who compromised intimacy with God. Generative themes allow us to see the telltale signs of humanity in our own life stories. They reveal truth about the consequences of sin and let in hope for those who struggle in the dark.

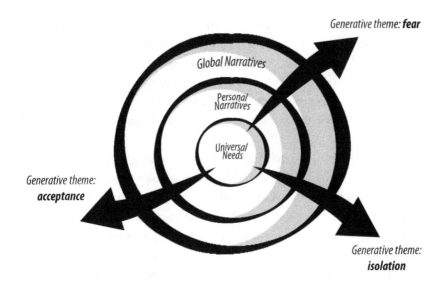

*Generative theme: **fear***

*Global Narratives*

*Personal Narratives*

*Universal Needs*

*Generative theme:* **acceptance**

*Generative theme:* **isolation**

As mentioned, generative themes help us link our lives to scripture. They reveal what we hope for, fear and assume about the world, God and other people. Once identified, they situate beliefs, contradictions and blind spots in a larger framework. In naming them and applying cultural, biblical and human insight, we see more of God and more about ourselves. Generative themes are broad, open and widely applicable. Because they describe the human condition, we can find passages of scripture that explore their significance and offer direction for the way forward out of the pig field.

In what follows, using two ministry case studies, generative themes are named and their inherent contradictions, beliefs and blind spots are pointed out. As part of theological reflection, while considering Freire's approach, you can see that generative themes contain universal needs, personal narratives, and global perspectives that inform the two ministry stories that follow.

### JAKE'S PRESENT

Jake wasn't sure anymore why he decided to be a pastor. At this point, the church was doing okay, it had been for several years now, but he thought he needed a bit of a boost, just the same. It was time for his denomination's annual meeting. He intended to go, this time without his wife. The meetings were in a large urban center, quite far from his small church community. He was tired and felt worn out. He thought some big city entertainment might help him get over the slump he felt he was in. Maybe it would help him forget about church problems for a while. Everyone was always after him, wanting him for one thing or another. He just needed a bit of a break—that was all.

Jake decided to drive the family van to the meetings because it would give him time to think things over, he told himself, several times. He raised his voice to his wife as she asked him why he was going alone, and taking the van, since it would be more economical if he went with the pastor from a nearby town. Their other car was not so dependable and she needed it to get the kids to school and get to work. He was a bit surprised at himself when he yelled, but it seemed to quiet the whole situation down. She said no more and said very little before he left. It was a nice change…he told himself.

As he was driving to the meetings he decided to stop for coffee and got out a city map. He recalled that someone joked about a section of town where prostitutes worked and where there was a series of strip clubs he'd driven past once when he was looking for an address. He thought he would just try to find that area to see if it was still the same. He wouldn't stop there. Of course not! He had never visited that sort of neighborhood before. He wouldn't go to a prostitute—what a crazy idea, though he might just stop in somewhere for a cup of coffee. He was in plenty of time to register for the meetings. He had left home early so he could see a bit of the city before he checked in at the conference hotel. He just wanted a bit of a change.

Once he got into the city, Jake drove slowly through the neighborhood he thought he recalled. He turned a corner and drove through a second time. He spotted a coffee shop. Well, he wanted a coffee. Anyway, he needed to use the washroom. He wouldn't stay long. He was headed for the conference. That was why he came after all. He chuckled to himself as he stopped the car and got out. "If anyone saw me...."

Some time later, Jake was having a drink in a strip club down the street from his parked car. The people seemed okay, no big deal. He sat for several hours watching the show. He would never go to a prostitute. He loved his wife. He really loved his wife very much. Suddenly, while standing at his elbow, a woman was pointing to the chair next to him, asking if she could sit down. He thought to himself that even if he said yes, it would only be for a little while. She looked as if she really wanted to talk to someone. Hours later, Jake stumbled back to his van. He sat behind the wheel, not really sure whether to start the engine or just sit there.

**Reflective Questions**

What's going on in this story? Right now, spend time and write out your reactions to the story. Please do this recording before you read any further. Be as explicit in what you think as you can.

This next section includes some insights into what's going on with Jake. This isn't the only way to interpret Jake's situation, but using reflective questions and the notion of generative themes, there are some plausible ways to think about what's going on with Jake.

Some of these insights about the case study come from giving it to students and hearing their responses. Students either feel sorry for him or abhor him. Reactions are strong. He throws them back on fears about themselves and they pity him, or he represents something they fear may happen to them or to their spouse. Either as Jake or his wife, they feel repulsed.

Discussing Jake's story can lead to two dead-ends that overly support or denounce his humanity. Both dead-ends dehumanize him, his wife and his church congregation. If we get into a dead-end reaction, we may be unable to hear scripture effectively. Some Christian leaders have said they can't find a single example of a good marriage in the Bible so, they imply, maybe a good marriage isn't possible for people in ministry. This belief is a dead-end. We arrive at dead-ends eventually if we refuse to identify contradictions inherent in case studies like this one. A dead-end results if we fail to identify contradictions inherent in Jake's story. For example we find that he:

- Loves his wife vs. Wants to be alone

- Loves his wife vs. Stops her from saying what she thinks

- Loves his wife vs. Drives to a strip club area and parks

- Thinks his church is doing okay vs. Needs a boost, a break, a change

- Leaves for the conference early to register vs. Looks for the neighborhood

- Doesn't go early to the conference vs. Drives slowly then stays in the strip club area

- Thinks visiting a prostitute is crazy vs. Invites a strange woman to sit beside him

If we're simply cynical about Jake, these issues won't appear to us as contradictions. We'll diminish one side of the debate and emphasize the other. But if we do that, we've given in to unhealthy reason and applied it to this situation. In so doing, we've shut down healthy theological reflection.

The narrative doesn't make clear what Jake did, so we don't know what happened. But we do know he's upset. Read Zechariah 3: 1-7 and imagine you're in the van with Jake. He's in the driver's seat. God is in the passenger seat. Satan is sitting on the first bench seat leaning forward between Jake and God—whispering. You're sitting at the back of the van. What do you think you'd hear in Satan's hoarse whispers? Remember that you're slightly removed, a bit distant from the conversation at the back of the van. It's helpful, as you focus on destabilizing experiences, to imagine you're somewhat distant so you can get a full view of everyone's interaction. You're inside the problem but have a bit of distance from what you're trying to focus on.

One possible generative theme in Jake's story is a culture of silence. He doesn't tell anyone what he's thinking or feeling. There's also deceit and subterfuge. Jake is working behind the scenes and doesn't discuss ministry with colleagues, marriage with his wife, despair and temptation with his friends. Like Cain, he's uncommunicative and alone.

A generative theme of silence can be explored psychologically, socially, culturally and biblically. We could gather expert opinion on a culture of silence in marriage, how it begins and what to do about it. We can find themes of silence in scripture: David walked alone on a wall and saw Bathsheba bathing when usually he'd be at war. David was involved in deceit and subterfuge; he invented a plan that led to Uriah's death. Cain was silent, as was the prodigal son—both refusing to question the status quo and failing to hear what God longed to teach—except the hard way. There's also a generative theme of sin. What does scripture say about sin? How does sin operate? What's the big picture we can piece together about sin? If we examine Jake's story without identifying its generative themes, we simply react to it using our pre-conceived ideas of the human condition, or of people 'like Jake'. We can't learn from destabilizing situations unless we unpack their generative themes.

Chapter One described theological reflection as a conversation that could become a dialogue. Dialogical theological reflection produces works such as Augustine's *Confessions*, Bunyan's *Pilgrim's Progress*, C.S. Lewis' *A Pilgrim's Regress* or Julian of Norwich's analysis of *Divine Love*. These reflections are satisfying conversations grounded in God's love, prayer and scripture that are applied to the whole of one's life, whether the authors tell the story in first or third person. Their works go very deep. They dig into contradictions and blind spots. Through conversation, God reveals blind spots and contradictions, sometimes with help from other people. With these books in mind, here's another piece of Jake's story.

JAKE'S PAST

Jake grew up in a home with parents who were busy most of the time. He had two younger sisters. He was fairly quiet as a small boy. He liked reading books, watching TV and playing with his dog. On one occasion, Jake and his family were having supper. His two sisters began fighting at the table over who had to clean off the dishes. They didn't fight openly with each other but were kicking each other under the table. One kick must have landed a serious blow because one of them started to scream. Jake's father had been eating his dinner and reading the paper at the same time. At the sound of the girl's scream, he leapt from the table and grabbed Jake by the arm. He dragged the boy to his room, hollering that Jake had no business disrupting supper. The family sat in silence as they heard Jake being beaten. Later, while in his room recovering, his father went outside in the backyard where he knew Jake could see him. The father held up Jake's dog by the scruff of its neck. Jake heard the dog whimpering and ran to the window in time to see his father let the dog go and take his rifle and shoot the dog.

**Reflective Questions**

What's going on in this story? Right now, spend time and write out your reactions to the story. Please do this recording before you read any further. Be as explicit in what you think as you can.

Jake's childhood has generative themes that include coercion and domination, carried out in a culture of silence. If much of what Jake believes about God and the church comes from his own experience rather than exposure to scripture, those who reflect theologically on his story need to add biblical, social, psychological and personal insight as they listen to it.

By analyzing the present moment we find ourselves in, we locate Jake in an adult culture that isn't coercive but permissive. He hasn't learned the self-regulation that allows someone to take action and communicate personal needs. His desire to do what he feels like doing has support from a social milieu that keeps telling him to look out for himself and be happy. In his cultural setting, as long as he doesn't hurt anyone else, it doesn't matter what he does on his own time. What are biblical passages that inform Jake's situation? How does scripture talk about power? How does God use power? What else do you understand about social power that might inform your understanding of Jake? How might aspects of a permissive culture interact with the pattern of coercion he grew up facing?

## FIGURE #1 HITTING THE TARGET

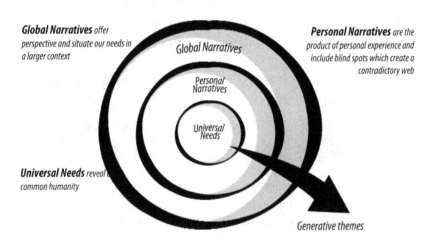

**Global Narratives** offer perspective and situate our needs in a larger context

**Personal Narratives** are the product of personal experience and include blind spots which create a contradictory web

Global Narratives

Personal Narratives

Universal Needs

**Universal Needs** reveal common humanity

Generative themes

To understand Jake's situation, we locate him in three concentric circles: universal needs, personal narratives and global perspectives. Given influences from his personal life (silence and coercion), adult culture (permissiveness) and a universal need (to be significant) Jake believes there are some things he can't do and some things it doesn't really matter if he does, at least, he wants to believe they don't matter. But if he were confident that private behaviour doesn't matter, he would make no effort to hide what he's doing.

Freire refers to beliefs such as these as untested feasibilities: something we believe we can't do but have never tried to do. At this point, Jake doesn't realize that his beliefs are untested feasibilities. As examples, according to the information we have in the scenario, he hasn't tried to speak truthfully to his wife, have friends in which to confide, or lead the church community toward genuine, godly success. These actions don't appear to him as options. If he tried to carry out these actions, he would have to master himself, to some extent. Recall that God told Cain he must master himself, something Cain saw as unfeasible. The prodigal son felt he couldn't stay at home. He didn't try to discover options; instead, he left. In situations that trap us, we discover what we think can't be done. If we uncover what seems unfeasible, we begin to reframe the way we think about the world and the possibility of transformation shows up.

Blind spots are often untested feasibilities, assumptions we don't know we hold—or that hold us back. Untested assumptions trap us in a situation in which it seems there's no way out. Jake isn't alone in feeling trapped. A second case study reveals other traps in the destabilizing situation that another leader has to face.

---

### MARJORIE'S PRESENT

Marjorie has an MDiv degree and is director of a church-based day care centre. She's been in this position for ten years. When she started at the centre she was a youth pastor. But she had plans for herself. She always dreamed of leading the best day care in the city and since she had been the director, her center set the pace for others. She knew people who had a direct line to funding agencies. If she wanted something, she knew she could get it.

Many of the children had been coming to the day care since infancy. She was committed to the families that came, especially those who helped her in various ways and supported her plans for improving the centre. She was able to ask people to go the second mile and loved the feeling that she could get people to carry out her plans. No one refused her. She believed it was because she was doing such a good job. She was well respected in the community. The evidence was in the certificates of excellence that hung on her walls.

Sometimes people got in the way. Often it was someone from the church who made a fuss about some little thing she was doing. There were few frustrations in her work because she could get most people to do what she wanted. If a staff member didn't comply, she could always fire that person. Generally, she looked after her staff members and they did what she said. Things ran pretty smoothly.

The church was a problem. They wanted to share space yet the day care rented it five days a week. Day care staff cared for it well and got funding for building improvements. Marjorie was sure the church could never have accomplished what the day care had done. Those church people didn't run their affairs with efficiency and expertise as she did. When she needed them to do something, it always took forever. They didn't keep promises of improving the site until she had to deal with them with some firmness. Mostly she just made them feel so good about helping, they eventually did what she asked. They weren't very clever really. If it weren't for her, the church would be in poor repair. She wondered if they appreciated what she did for them.

Recently she had seen a beautiful day care facility and knew her children deserved the quality surroundings the other day care had secured. She saw a need for new furniture, imagining colours that would look great with the furniture she had already. The children and families that came would enjoy the whole experience much more if she could get new furniture and equipment.

The staff seemed tired, some were sick, so she had a hard time getting enthusiasm when she mentioned the project at their staff meeting. They would have to do more fund raising, selling chocolates, baked goods—but they were so good at that she told them. This time she couldn't go to the city for money since bureaucrats tended to see this sort of thing as a luxury, which it wasn't. She felt angry that they saw it that way. It wasn't fair really. All she was trying to do was create a beautiful place for the children. It made her mad when people stood in her way. Other people had no vision. If they really cared, they'd see how important this new equipment was to her reputation for excellence.

**Reflective Questions**

What's going on in this story? Right now, spend time and write out your reactions. Please do this recording before you read any further. Be as explicit in what you think as you can. Focus on finding generative themes. Name the contradictions in Marjorie's story? What might be some of her blind spots?

Imagine you're in the van with Marjorie this time on her way home. What's destabilizing her? Reconstruct the scene you imagined with Jake, God and Satan. What would God be saying to Marjorie? What would Satan say to her? How might you think through Marjorie's perspective without speaking to her as Satan does? Imagine being in the van observing her compassionately to consider her situation. Try to hear what's going on and why she feels compelled to act the way she does.

In every human story there's a past, present and future. As observers of the story, we seldom have access to the trajectory of the life represented in the piece we see of it. In the generative themes and concentric circles that influence Marjorie, we see a universal precious and fragile longing to make a difference in the world that she tries to carry out in a culture of permissiveness. The following scenario expands on the present situation she finds herself in.

### MARJORIE'S PAST

You're walking with some friends through a shopping mall. Just ahead of you is a family consisting of a mother, father and little girl, perhaps three years of age. The mother and father have stopped to talk to two other adults. It looks to you as though the four of them are good friends. At any rate, all four are engrossed in the conversation. Next to the spot where they're visiting, the little girl is playing by a fountain. There's a sculpture in the middle of the fountain. The water is about one-half metre deep toward the middle.

You stop and watch as the little girl begins to play on edge of the fountain. As she's playing along the fountain edge, she speaks loudly to her parents. You wonder whether you should do something. The mother turns from her conversation and says "Get down from there." You look back at the child and somehow you don't think the child will get down. The mother looks at the child and returns to the conversation, this happens two or three times. The father looks up once and raises his voice: "Get down, Marjorie." The child stops for a moment. The father waits. Then she bends down to get off the ledge. The father turns back to the conversation. The girl straightens up and continues to walk along the fountain's edge. Suddenly, she slips, falling in the pool. Everyone is very upset. Her parents are angry.

**Reflective Questions**

What's going on in this story? Right now, spend time and write out your reactions to it. Please do this recording before you read any further. Be as explicit in what you think as you can. Again, consider the contradictions and generative themes that are present in this story.

One way to understand the story is to identify the generative theme of parental neglect and permissiveness. Children of neglect tend to find it impossible to respect other people and don't know how to establish and maintain appropriate boundaries. If Marjorie read some of the books on leadership, she might assume she's an ideal leader and feel justified in how she operates. She's visionary, action-oriented and growth-producing. What more could anyone ask?

But, like Jake, she is an isolated leader. What then is required of theological reflection? We suggest it's necessarily collaborative because people like you and me, Jake and Marjorie, need others to come alongside and help identify patterned behaviour that keeps us isolated and unable to learn from life experience to be more like Jesus Christ. In collaboration, we gain insight from scripture by appropriating its meaning and applying it effectively to our lives.

## WITNESSES TO A CONVERSATION

As outlined in Artful Listening, witnesses help us hear our own life story in a new way. We need to hear what our companions in the back of the van see and hear when we talk about destabilizing events that erupt in ministry and seem to make no sense. We need witnesses to help us get some distance (at the back of the van) with regard to our destabilizing issues. Witnesses listen to present and past experiences in a way that permits the one who struggles to see the future in a new way. Witnesses co-investigate with us when they

- Intercede in prayer as they listen
- Listen artfully
- Suspend their personal interpretations
- Resist reason that belittles, analyzes, blames, suppresses, lectures or drowns
- Try to comprehend the whole story and its meaning
- Participate compassionately on the strength of their personal experience
- Name generative themes
- Suggest universal needs, personal narratives, and global perspectives
- Attend to differences between their experience and the one they're hearing
- Identify contradictions by helping a speaker see them for himself or herself
- Empathize by describing the narrative to the satisfaction of the narrator
- Sympathize (when possible) with the sensibility of the speaker
- Resonate with the generative theme if possible
- Probe what might be a blind spot, but not simply by naming it
- Tell the truth

In the previous chapter, Artful Listening was described in terms of an encounter between two people, but the practice also informs theological reflection when its done in a group. The list above relies for its backdrop on a group of people expert in Artful Listening.

In the presence of Artful Listening, employing the arts of theological reflection, dialogue with those who come alongside has potential to open up the future to real change. People don't change without going deeper in dialogue with God, themselves and others. It's hard to change if we can't see what we're currently doing and sense how it fails to conform to our own values. We need to see generative themes, contradictions and blind spots in our life stories as they're held up in the presence of others who know how to create a safe space.

Theological reflection is a practice that invites us to speak the truth in love. It's not talk that tells others what we think of them. It reveals inner struggles in a speaker who's given the full attention of witnesses who listen compassionately. Speaking the truth in love lets us hear ourselves in an atmosphere of love and healthy reason.

After we're aware of generative themes, contradictions, blind spots that show up in destabilizing events, we move to deeper understanding of the worldview that we hold as it currently shapes how we do ministry. Our purpose is to connect with scripture so we can see what Christian maturity is like and recognize a way out of traps we find ourselves in.

The goal of theological reflection is friendship with God. Like experienced monks, we want to enjoy God and love him forever. We want to see God's glory reflected in our lives and ministry. We want to have inner peace that conveys God's Presence. So we co-operate with God by doing spiritual work that produces the fruit of the Spirit in a life of faith. The next section draws attention to the personal work that's involved in theological reflection and offers a framework for a personal worldview inventory. The section offers specific tools for doing the personal spiritual work that's necessary as people engage in theological dialogue that's designed to help them mature as followers of the Lord Jesus Christ.

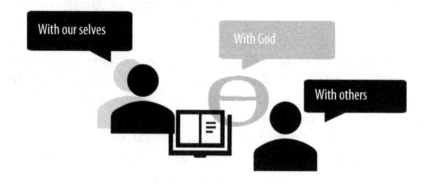

## PERSONAL INQUIRY

The first chapter referred to personal and collaborative inquiry as aspects of theological reflection and introduced the basic practice of *Lectio Divina*. This section provides further background on *Lectio Divina* and personal inquiry that's possible through its practice. In this chapter, personal inquiry may be carried out with others present, but it's primarily concerned with observing the movement of one's own soul. Without personal, spiritual effort in practices like *Lectio Divina*, theological reflection is shallow and ad hoc. It's only through intentional, determined, prayerful reflection that theological insight is effectively brought to bear on the circumstances faced in ministry.

Henry Nouwen suggested the original meaning of the word theology was 'union with God in prayer'.[1] Early church fathers and mothers engaged in reflection and prayer simultaneously. The connection between thinking and praying is important for us to understand as well as to practice. Pre-modern Christians reflected theologically according to a pattern of *Lectio Divina* or sacred reading that united prayer and thought in soulful thinking as described in chapter two. For those engaged in *Lectio Divina*, theological reflection was a form of devotion to God; loving God and thinking of God weren't separate activities: "their theology [was] continually rising up into prayer" with "no distinction between the two [so that] theology was a hymn, a prayer, the point where knowledge and love become praise."[2]

As one example, Anselm (1033-1109)[3] wrote devotionally and theologically. Along with other pre-moderns, the form and emotion of his devotional poems weren't separate. The practice of meditative prayer, *Lectio Divina*, was ancient by the time he began to write. He introduced innovations to unite spiritual purification and intellectual illumination. In what follows, there's an elaborated second strategy for *Lectio Divina*, which introduces *sapientia* into the four movements of its traditional method. Introducing *sapientia* enables twenty-first century believers to address adverse effects of modern prejudices about the role of reason. As mentioned, pre-modern monks understood the role of reason in a way that modernity eclipsed.

By proposing a second way to carry out theological reflection based on *Lectio Divina*, there's no intention to replace the traditional practice. The emphasis is on an aspect of devotional theological reflection that's spelled out for the times we live in. Sometimes the Expanded version will be helpful; sometimes the traditional one will be the most useful.

As mentioned, there are four stages to the pattern: *lectio, meditatio, oratio, contemplatio*. It's a very old method used by monastic orders, and generally associated with John Cassian of the fifth century. *Lectio Divina* was used for centuries to enrich heart-filled devotion to God. During its practice, someone reads a passage several times with different purposes. To the medieval mind, reading was an action of the whole person. The text was read until it was absorbed, just as food is absorbed into the body for nourishment so the body can continue to have life.

Scripture was memorized, providing a framework for building personal worldviews. Scripture says, taste and see that the Lord is good! *Lectio Divina* was frequently compared to eating: "Taste by reading, chew by understanding, swallow by loving and rejoicing" so that the scripture "'O taste and see how gracious the Lord is' was applied more often to the reading of scripture than to the Eucharist before the twelfth century."[4]

*Lectio Divina* is described somewhat differently in recent

work. The practice itself needs to be adapted to our times. In its historical context

> The goal of this monastic approach to prayer and study was to help the believer experience, and not just intellectually understand, God as the object of scripture. This manner of study includes four steps: *Lectio* -meaning active reading, in which the words were spoken aloud so that they would engage the body, the lips and ears, not just the mind; *Meditatio* -during which the words were repeated and ruminated upon with the goal of fixing them in one's memory in the hope that one's thoughts and will would be shaped by them; *Oratio* -a response to God in which one shares with God not just thoughts, but one's emotions regarding the text; and *Contemplatio* -the attempt to quiet oneself and commune with God, to allow God and the work of the previous three steps to speak to one's heart.[5]

The goal of the basic practice was to unite the human spirit with the Holy Spirit in a way that allowed a follower of Jesus to observe the movement of the soul. In that process, what's the role played by these two agents of communication? How does it work between the human and Holy Spirit as they commune with one another?

### THE HUMAN SPIRIT AND THE HOLY SPIRIT

The beginning of the book asserts that theological reflection is carried out with help from the Holy Spirit. The scriptural relationship between the Holy Spirit and the human spirit marks off how they work together during theological reflection. This relationship, as agents of communication, is the foundation for the meaningful spiritual work that's done during theological reflection. How, then, does the human spirit connect with the Holy Spirit? While they're as different from one another as humanity differs from God, they work together because they have the same function: the human spirit and Holy Spirit are the means of communication between humanity and God.

In scripture, terms that describe the Holy Spirit also apply to the human spirit. In the New Testament (NRSV) there are 338 references to the word spirit or spirits. Functions of spirit are named that cohere around its capacity as an agent of communication. The Spirit indwells (Rom. 8:11), bears witness (Rom. 8:16), intercedes (Rom. 8:26), advocates (John 15:26), directs (Acts 11:12), prays (Eph. 6:18), interprets (1Cor. 2:13), reveals (1 Tim. 3:16), yearns (James 4:5), speaks (Rev. 2:11), strengthens (Rom. 8:26), guides (Gal. 5:25), unifies (1 Cor. 6:17), comforts (Acts 9:31), confirms truth (Rom. 9:1) and conveys Presence (Col. 2:5). Romans 8:27 says that God who searches our hearts knows the mind of the Spirit and the Spirit intercedes for the saints in accordance with God's will. The Holy Spirit connects humanity with God and is the agent of communication within the Holy Trinity.

In their capacity for communication, the human spirit and the Holy Spirit are significant in relationship to one another and establish a link described in parental terms. The human spirit is an aspect of what it means to be a person; the human spirit has a Father in God. Jesus distinguishes between those whose Father is the devil and those whose Father is God. (Matt. 10:20) In a Christian worldview, the human spirit isn't simply good or neutral; it's connected to its Father. The outcome of that connection is evidenced in the life a person leads so that spirituality shapes morality. Our sense of connection to others, and a feeling of obligation for the way we treat them, are directed by spiritual experience and assumptions and beliefs derived though that experience.

Christian mythology or cosmology (a worldview or grand narrative) is an interpretation of the universe as a whole. Myth is discussed more fully in the following chapter. At this point, it's important to provide a context for the relationship between the human spirit and the Holy Spirit[6] by pointing out that scripture describes a spiritual kingdom that includes the following participants: the human spirit, the Holy Spirit, unclean spirits, demons, Your Father (the devil), Abba, Father (God), spirits of the prophets, spirits of the dead, foul spirits, elemental spirits of the world or the spirit of the world. It would seem that every person has a spirit but people can become unspiritual, (1Cor. 2:14) that is, dull to spiritual urgings.

The spiritual kingdom is inhabited by angels (Heb. 1:14), which are messengers of God, as well as demons, unclean or evil spirits led by Satan. Christians are emboldened to stand against devilish schemes and recognize these enemies are spiritual not human. Scripture states that "our struggle is not against flesh and blood, but against the rulers, against the authorities, against the spiritual forces of evil in the heavenly realms" (Eph. 6:12). The spiritual kingdom is multi-layered and scripture affirms the human spirit's strength to resist the enemy due to the power and presence of God. As James 4:8b says: "Resist the devil, and he will flee from you. Come near to God and he will come near to you."

People are influenced spiritually by their interpretation of the cosmological order of things, or by the story they tell about the world as a whole. Christian cosmology differs from secular and materialistic views, as well as from other religious perspectives. This is important to realize.

It's also important to recognize that the spiritual aspect of humanity is universal: everyone is spiritual whether or not she or he is religious. Spirituality is formed through five dimensions of ordinary experience, namely biological, cultural, sociological, neurological and psychological processes. The psychological aspect is referred as object relations theory which unified the other four dimensions.

At the heart of spiritual experience is gaze behaviour between mother and child that initiates the inter-subjective experience of infants, introducing them to personal, spiritual and material worlds they inhabit for the rest of their lives. Spiritual dimensions of personal experience generate a personal worldview that people form and that conveys to them life's meaning, its possibilities and its limitations.

In general, the five dimensions help to form these personal worldviews (or narratives) in the following ways:

- Biology influences survival and suggests whether the world is friendly or not

- Culture transmits spiritual data to children through memes

- Sociology suggests the need to fit in and distinguish ourselves from the world
- Genetic research implies that the brain is hard-wired for religion
- Psychology explains object relations theories

The human spirit builds a framework for making life meaningful through these five processes. A sense of felt connection arises multi-dimensionally from birth. Object relating (the making of meaning) shapes spirituality and identity. Under favourable conditions, spirituality expresses itself relationally and conversationally; if it finds ways to flourish, it can strengthen personal identity in a positive way.

Whether or not conditions are favourable, the outcome of spiritual experience is the formation of a personal worldview each of us has by early adolescence. If spirituality is neglected, we form impoverished worldviews that can't sustain us through crises of ordinary living; we don't feel well connected to God, the world, others or ourselves if spiritual needs are unmet.

Spiritual poverty is an atrophied sense of felt connection and occurs because making meaning isn't simply a personal project. Environments in which spirituality flourishes or fails are crucial. A spiritual environment is created and sustained in families of origin. Families are nested within larger social, cultural, gender, racial and economic frameworks so that worldviews are shaped by what we experience globally, not only culturally and in the family.

Theological reflection dips into these worldviews as it works with the assumptions and expectations generated by them. Effective theological dialogue provides a healthy environment for spirituality to flourish so that worldviews can be revised according to scripture, Christian tradition and the community of saints. The whole point of conversation that becomes dialogue is realized in the possibility of allowing what we think now, based on our experience, to be refined and transformed by the Living God, in company with other believers.

### FIGURE #2 TRANSMITTING

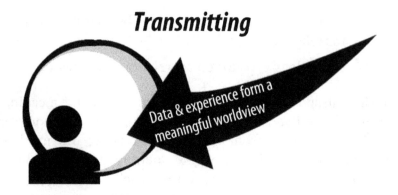

*Transmitting*

Data & experience form a meaningful worldview

Through the five sets of spiritually formative processes named above (biology, culture, sociology, neurology and psychology) a worldview gradually forms in every human being.

---

**Questions for Reflection**

- Did you grow up with a sense of plenty or poverty?

- Describe some people, places, events or things that you feel deeply connected to?

- What do you think it means to have no other gods before God?

- What are some of the struggles you've had or still have with competing gods?

- Write down some questions this section raises for you about human spirituality.

- If you rated yourself on your freedom to speak to other people about God using a scale of 1 to 10, with 1 being completely uncomfortable, 5 being sometimes comfortable, and 10 being always comfortable, what would that number be?

- In discussing the relationship between the human spirit and the Holy Spirit, people who reflect theologically need consciously to invite the Holy Spirit into the process. If you rely on the image of God standing with Joshua and inviting Satan to see Joshua compassionately, what does that scripture convey to you about God's friendliness?

- We know we're supposed to believe that God's love for us is vast, immeasurable. What is your feeling when you imagine God in the van with you?

It's our full assurance of God's love for us that allows us to enter into theological reflection in a way that engages our freedom to emerge from the experience as renewed people, capable and willing to be more like Jesus.

In what follows, we invite you to consider carefully some of the tools that allow us to reflect on the current concepts we have for God, some of which might hinder us from seeing God's fullness, friendliness and mercy.

## TOOLS FOR THINKING ABOUT GOD

In general, whether we reflect with other people or in solitude, we bring God's presence and purpose to bear on thoughts, feelings and actions we're considering. Through prayer, we invite the Holy Spirit to inform our inquiry and intentions that arise from theological work. When we reflect collaboratively, we engage in a form of intercessory prayer in which we consciously and intentionally try to hear the Holy Spirit and other people as they voice their experience. We listen with attitudes that honour God and are informed by God's heart.

In hearing others, we recall Jesus' words: out of the overflow of the heart the mouth speaks (Matthew 12:34b). As we attend to others, we try to perceive what's on their heart and what's in our own heart. As we listen, we continuously correct our perceptions by prayerfully asking God to allow us to hear the other person as opposed to being distracted by our own ideas about what they mean, as outlined in Artful Listening. In listening, we suspend our own theories so we can genuinely hear what another is saying. We don't abandon our own theories about God or human experience, but we wait attentively until we sense what the other person wants to convey. All this listening is couched in prayer.

### REFLECTING ON GOD-CONCEPTS

A common way to describe theological reflection is by using the phrase 'faith seeking understanding,' as employed by Duke and Stone referred to in chapter one. The expression needs some unpacking.

What's implied by the word faith? Does it refer to personal faith in God? Can people without faith in God carry out theological reflection? Notice how this way of speaking about theological reflection differs from *Lectio Divina*. There's no indication that prayer or communing with God is implicit in the process, which isn't to say we should refrain from using the expression. We want to reiterate the view that prayer and sacred reading of scripture are essential starting points for theological reflection and to say that seeking understanding is also dependent on sustained, prayerful meditation on scripture. Faith that seeks understanding must be rooted in devotion if it would grow to maturity.

In general, what is faith? Every human being has faith in something or someone and is compelled to exercise faith if they are emotionally well. In addition, everyone has a concept for God, whether or not they're believers. Ana Maria Rizzuto, psychologist and psychoanalyst, identified four primary God concepts through her research with patients and hospital personnel. The four God concepts include those who

- Have a God whose existence they don't doubt

- Wonder whether or not to believe in a God they aren't sure exists

- Are amazed, angered, or quietly surprised to see others deeply invested in a God that doesn't interest them

- Struggle with a demanding, harsh God they'd like to get rid of if they weren't convinced of God's existence and power [7]

During collaborative reflection, wisdom from above (James 3:17) requires us to respond to people differently depending on the God concept already formed in their thinking. It's these personal God concepts that theological reflection challenges. If we work collaboratively with others, we must pay attention to how they conceive God. For example, if our concept is that God is kind and loving, we find it hard to connect with someone who sees God as harsh and wishes they could eradicate this painful idea from their thought life. We must be patient with these differences.

People arrive at God concepts through experience. When we collaborate, we ask with compassion about experiences with significant people (without being intrusive) to hear their idea of God and gain some insight into our own concept of God as well. It's beneficial to be with people who aren't the same as us. Their differences help us hear our own concepts in a new way, as long as we try to hear each other rather than impose a view of God on the other. We don't have to agree with someone to hear them effectively. Our worldview can be instructive to others but not if it's forced on them. Scripture tells us not to argue but to present the faith with gentleness and respect.

Individual concepts for God are aspects of theological reflection that create dissonance in a group. Naming them is an important part of the process. In the parable of the talents, (Matthew 25:14-30) the one-talent man hid his talent because he viewed God as a tyrant. He acted out of a concept for God that paid out in experience: he got what he expected.

Expectations of God are generated by God concepts. We can submit these concepts to God and compare them with scripture. If we refuse to submit our current concepts, we're spiritually blind. Spiritual blindness is designed blindness (a blind spot) inherent in a personal or communal worldview if it holds to a concept for God and refuses to open to new insight from God. The man born blind (John 9:13-41) uncovers spiritual blindness in the Pharisees who could not see Jesus as Messiah. In their case, they were sure they knew what Messiah would do for them; their expectations of Messiah prevented them from connecting God with Jesus. (John 7:25-29)

---

**Questions for Reflection**

In order to reflect on your current God concept and consider the content of your personal worldview, jot down your responses to the following questions.

- What do you think God is like?
- What's the tone of God's voice as God speaks to you?
- What's the look on God's face when God looks at you?
- Are there people in your life that seem to see God in different ways than you do?
- How do you usually feel around them? What are you often thinking when you're with them?
- Is there something you long to believe about God, but can't seem to manage?
- What are you hoping for in your relationship with God?

On the basis of this initial recording of your current thinking, as best you can write it down, take an inventory of the personal worldview you've organized as a way of making meaning out of personal, communal and social experience.

---

# Notes

1. Henry Nouwen, *In the Name of Jesus* (New York: Crossroad, 1989), 30.
2. *St. Anselm*, 44.

3.  *St Anselm*, Introduction.

4.  *St Anselm*, 53.

5.  Dorothy Hunse, "Julian of Norwich—Her experience of Grace and Ours." Unpublished manuscript and paper presented to the Canadian Evangelical Theological Association (May) 2007 at the University of Saskatchewan in Saskatoon, Saskatchewan.

6.  The Holy Spirit, uncapitalized, is mentioned 3 times in the Old Testament: Psalm 51:11, Isaiah 63:10-11 but is emphasized throughout the New Testament and referenced 338 times in the New Revised Standard Version.

7.  Ana Maria Rizzuto, *The Birth of the Living God*, (Chicago: Chicago University Press, 1979), 181.

CHAPTER 5

# NARRATIVE INQUIRY AND
# THEOLOGICAL REFLECTION

A s mentioned in the previous chapter, personal worldviews are set in frameworks of meaning that are larger than anyone's individual meaning system. They're like personal mental mythologies set in a larger mythology about the world. The word *myth* may confuse people. Modern Christian culture, like modern secular culture, tends to misunderstand the word. Earlier a broad Christian worldview was referred to as a cosmology or mythology. These two terms are used as synonyms in this chapter. What, then, is myth?

In this chapter, the first section explores the word myth as it relates to the life stories we live by. Following that section, there are opportunities to consider how you think about the world, yourself, God and other people by answering the questions provided. You won't be asked to share your answers to these questions with other people, although you will be invited to reflect on patterns you see in the story you tell about life. The purpose of the chapter is to describe how myth functions and to see how the story you tell yourself and other people is part of the greater myth that shapes how you think and act and also reveals what you bring to theological reflection. The purpose is to glimpse your own worldview and to consider how it influences the way you read scripture and the way you engage in theological reflection.

As an example, Pharisees in Jesus' day held to a myth about the world that included their expectation that Messiah would come. Answers to questions of who he would be, how he would come and what he would accomplish were embedded in their mythological conception that was built on their understanding of scripture and experience, for example, on the historical event of release from captivity in Egypt. For them, the myth they lived by didn't allow them to recognize him as Messiah even though Jesus tried to help them see how the Old Testament story pointed to him. Their myths were dissonant with the Old Testament (e.g., the truth about Messiah). In another example, the one-talent man (Matthew 25:14-30) held to a personal myth that contained a harsh, punitive God. As a result, he reacted to his one talent by hiding it, an action congruent with the four God concepts in the previous chapter in Rizzuto's research, specifically in the fourth option for God concepts, i.e., those who hold the concept that God is harsh.

We react to God based on what we think God's like. Theological reflection is an opportunity to reconsider God concepts in order to know God more fully, which is why reflecting theologically is necessarily rooted in scripture, a faith community, worship and devotion. As a result of its role in the way we think about God, myth also plays a role in theological reflection. Why is this so?

Christian scripture has been a significant, dominant myth for two thousand years. To call the Bible a myth, isn't to say it's untrue; not at all. The word myth doesn't mean that the Bible is untrue in total or in any of its parts; it means the opposite. It's entirely true in its parts, as a whole and in it's function to inform our own worldviews and transform them based on its truthfulness. The Bible is more than merely true; it tells us what's real. Myth operates in the realm of imagination. While reason tells us what's true, imagination shows us what is real. What's real forms a basis for making meaning, not simply what's true at a particular time, in a particular place, among a particular group of people.

Recall that we know only in part, not the whole. Reality, in contrast, is a large, permanent framework that stands behind what we hold to be true. Reality is multi-dimensional. Only God sees and knows it fully. Hence, revelation from God allows us to see beyond our finite capacity to perceive the world. Myth always calls forth belief. What's meant if we say that myth is relevant to theological reflection? What can we learn about the nature and function of myth that helps us do better theological reflection? Further, what are we implying by saying that the biblical text is contains myth and that myth is true?

As Levi-Strauss (a linguist who was the most prominent exponent of structuralism) put it, science has only two ways of proceeding as it tries to understand a text. It can use either reductionism or structuralism. Reductionism is an approach to text that takes very complex phenomena, which the biblical text is, and reduces them to simpler phenomena at a simpler level of analysis.[1] A bible scholar, for example, might take a portion of scripture and reduce it to a simpler phenomenon in the sense that he or she separates it out and investigates it without reference to its connection to the whole Bible. Reductionist analyses can be applied to complex phenomena when someone tries to gain understanding, but something is lost or remains unexplained at the end of a reductionist approach.

For example, we might examine bits of the lost son story in scripture and realize the extent to which he dishonoured his father by asking for his inheritance while the father was still alive. But after we acquire that data, we can always ask—so what! How does that insight apply to my life and how does that help me understand what God requires of me? We ask 'so what' questions since theological reflection is always meant to lead us to the living God, Jesus Christ. It's not just an historical analysis or contextual examination. Jesus is alive now and intercedes for us with the Father. The educational aim of theological reflection is always to apply scripture to life.

The second scientific approach to text is structuralism and from this point of view calling the biblical text a myth is most revealing. Structuralism refers to keeping a text as a whole entity. When we approach complex phenomena that can't be reduced to a lower level of meaning without losing something essential, we do so by seeing the interplay of relationships within the text and by trying to understand it as a system (possibly by trying to understand it in its original form as a system).

When we try to comprehend complex phenomena as a whole we're often drawn to analogies for explanation. The idea of myth is an analogy for the biblical text as whole and it holds up only to the extent that it's a good analogy. Levi-Strauss makes clear that myth itself is a complex phenomenon and uses an analogy of music to help explore myth; for us by extension, music and myth help to understand how to use scripture during theological reflection. So how does it all work?

Levi-Strauss used music to say that myth can't be read in a linear fashion. Myth must be apprehended as a totality. How does his point inform theological reflection? Reading myth isn't like reading newspapers or novels that we read from beginning to end, left to right, and then are done with when we know how it ends. Myth is total, not linear. The basic meaning of myth isn't conveyed by a sequence of events but by "bundles of events" even though these events appear at different moments in the overall narrative."[2] He suggests that we read myth like we listen to an orchestral score, "not stave after stave, but understanding that something which was written on the first stave at the top of the page acquires meaning only if one considers that it is part and parcel of what is written below, on the second stave, the third stave, and so on."[3]

Only by treating myth as a totality in which each part remains available to explain other parts, do we understand how scripture operates from a structuralist perspective. There is therefore, "a kind of continuous reconstruction taking place in the mind of the listener to music or the listener to a mythical story."[4] Reading myth isn't only a means of understanding a whole view of the world, its function is also to preserve that world so that "the future will remain faithful to the present and to the past."[5] While history can be revised, myth cannot; rather, we get deeper into its meaning as we get fuller access to the whole counsel of God. Aptly understood, myth "puts us in the correct spiritual or psychological posture for right action, in this world or the next."[6]

Myth not only conserves its own narrative, it also preserves its morality.

Theological reflection then, is a process of reconstruction in which we bring current God concepts and expectations for Christian life and ministry under the sovereignty of the whole biblical narrative, with help from the Holy Spirit who speaks with the human spirit.

We use the metaphor of myth to explain work that needs to be done in theological reflection. Narrative theological reflection is a well-known feature of ancient Near Eastern literature, which, from a Jewish perspective, ranges from earliest times through to rabbinic Midrash (i.e., inquiry, "interpretation to draw out meanings from a text" or to go beyond the plain sense of the text).[7] Narrative theological methods derive their substance from structuralist approaches to scripture.

Narrative theology and narrative approaches to theological reflection have features that are important to note, for example:

- More than one account of an event may be given

  - (e.g., two accounts of the creation of humanity (Gen. 1:26-31; Gen. 2:4-25) and

  - two accounts of Abram/Abraham passing Sarah off as his sister (Gen. 12:10-20; 20:1-18; cf. 26:1-1)

- The existence of variation isn't seen as a serious defect in the narrative

- Rigid consistency isn't essential to storytelling

- Redactors (editors) chose an approach in which they refused to discard variants as inauthentic or inaccurate, but saw them as sequential parts of a longer story

- There's repetition that serves to provide a rich and sophisticated presentation of themes

- These repetitions are seen as ripe with analogy that reveal, echo and suggest subtlety of interpretation

- They pile up on one another to deepen meaning rather than to create contradictions that must be cancelled out for coherent meaning to emerge

- There's a subtlety and richness that also applies to the mind of God[8]

In narrative reflection, something is caught by a story that can't be conveyed in a statement or proposition about God or human experience. The meaning of a story stays with us and continues to reveal what God is like and what's required of believers.

In theological reflection, we hear our own stories and those of other people. Through conversing together, and within ourselves, we place our narratives next to the story of God's action in the world—action that describes God's nature. In setting our story beside God's story, we choose whether our current narrative is one we want to keep telling or whether our story needs to change. Again, if change is chosen, we engage prayerfully together in God's name, through the power of the Holy Spirit to become more like Christ.

**Questions for Reflection**

- Do you struggle with using the word myth? What's the nature of that struggle?

- What is the main story that you tell about God?

- Are there stories about God that other people tell that make you uncomfortable'?

- What is the main story about God in the Old Testament?

- What is the main story about God in the New Testament'?

- Is there a story you tell about God but have trouble believing in yourself?

## PERSONAL INVENTORY OF A WORLDVIEW

In a private notebook write answers to as many of the following questions as you can. Theological reflection requires us to ask classic questions that have been raised about God over time. It also helps find answers we can apply to ourselves.

The questions from this inventory are adapted from many sources and start with common questions people ask about God, Jesus and Holy Spirit, as well as about themselves, other people and Christian community. There are questions about God that are raised in the Bible. For example, the disciples ask Jesus three questions during the upper room dialogues (John 17) before Jesus' arrest, crucifixion and resurrection. As we read that passage we not only identify our own deep search for Messiah but also hear Jesus' answers first-hand. There are two benefits to reading Jesus' answers: we get the content, the actual answers, and also perceive how he tended to answer questions. (John 14:5-31) Please read this passage, identify the questions and consider how he answered his disciples. What do you notice about Jesus' answers?

---

**Questions for Reflection**

In what follows, you have a list of basic questions that have been raised about God.[9] In theological reflection, personal and collaborative, it's significant to ask basic questions sincerely so that personal narratives can be brought into contact with the living Christian tradition. Take an extended time and record in your notebook answers to the following questions. Let your answers be as full as you can make them.

- What is the character of this universe in which we dwell?

- Does God influence every action or is God in control of what happens in a general way?

- What do you long for? Where and when is it?

- Why do people suffer if God is Love?

- Why do people hurt each other? Why do people help each other?

- Why do you hurt people? Why do you help people?
- Why do you hurt yourself? Why do you help yourself?
- What is beautiful to you? What terrifies you?
- What do you think God is doing (or wants to convey) in the situation you are facing?
- What is Jesus like?
- What is God like?
- What is prayer? How does prayer work?
- What is your life on earth for? What is your body for?
- How do you think about your own death?
- What makes an ordinary day pleasant for you?
- What use should we make of the world?
- How do you imagine Heaven? How do you imagine Hell?
- What are your favourite objects? Why do your favourite objects matter to you?
- Where are your favourite places? Where are your frightening places?
- What does it mean to be a spiritual person?
- What does it mean to be a religious person?
- What does it mean to be a good person?
- Who is your spiritual hero? What is this person like?
- What do you not want to be like?
- What human characteristics are you trying to avoid?
- When do you feel closest to God? Why? Where do you feel closest to God?
- What would you lose if you made God more central in your life?
- What would you gain if you made God more central in your life?

- What image describes life in general?

- What does (an important word) mean to you as you see it in scripture?

- What are the core concepts of the Christian faith – the essentials?

- What is Christian community like at its best?

---

**EXERCISE: PLEASE TAKE TIME TO DRAW A PICTURE OF GOD**

---

**EXERCISE: GOD CONCEPT INVENTORY**

In the same notebook, write down your own views by filling in the space left by the three dots in each statement, in all the following questions:

- I feel/do not feel close to God because...

- I felt closest to God was when I was __ years old because...

- In general, God is pleased/displeased with me/people because...

- God wants/does not want me to be good because...

- I believe/do not believe in a personal God because...

- I felt distant from God when I was __ because...

- My most important responsibilities toward God are...

- Love of God towards me is/is not important because...

- My love for God is/is not important because...
- The feeling I get/used to get from my relationship with God is one of __ because...
- Fear of God is/is not important because...
- What I like most about God is __ because...
- What I resent most about God is __ because...
- What I like/dislike most about my religious community is/was __ because...
- Emotionally, I would like to know that God feels __ for me because...
- Out of the religious characters I know, I would like to be like __ because...
- My favourite Bible character is __ because...
- I believe/do not believe in the devil because...
- If the devil exists, he wants us to __ because...
- I have/have not felt that I hated God because...
- God expects me to __ because...
- I feel that to obey the Commandments is/is not important because...
- I pray/do not pray because I feel that God will...
- God punishes/does not punish you if you – because...
- God considers my sin as __ because...
- I think the way God punishes people is __ because...
- I believe the way God rewards people is __ because...
- I think God provides/does not provide for my needs because...
- The most important thing I expect from God is __ because...
- For me to completely please God I would have to __ because....
- If I could change my past, I would __ because....

- If I could change myself now, I would __ because….
- If I am in distress, I turn/do not turn to God because…
- If I am happy, I thank/do not thank God because…
- If I received an absolute proof that God doesn't exist, I would __ because…
- Christianity has/has not helped me to live because…
- Prayer is/is not important to me because…
- I wish/do not wish to be with God after I die because…
- God is closest to those who _ because…
- I consider God as my __ because…
- God sees me as __ because…
- Given my experiences, I would describe God as __ because…
- The day I changed my way of thinking about God was __ because…
- Christian faith was always/never/at one time important to me because…
- For me, the world has/has not an explanation for its existence without God because…
- Once, when I thought about God…

**EXERCISE: PLEASE TAKE TIME TO DRAW A PICTURE OF YOUR FAMILY**

**EXERCISE: FAMILY INVENTORY**

In the same notebook, write down your views by filling in the blank on all the questions about family

- In my family I feel/felt closest to my __ because...
- I feel/felt distant from my __ because...
- I love/loved __ the most because...
- I dislike/disliked __ the most because she/ he...
- Physically/ Emotionally, I resemble my __ because...
- The general emotional tone of my family was...
- The favourite family member is/was my __ because...
- The family member I admire most is/was my __ because...
- The general conversation in my family was negative/positive...
- The family member I despise/despised the most is/was __ because...
- The family member I feared most is/was __ because...
- The boss in my family is/was my __ because...
- The disciplinarian in my family is/was my __ because...
- The provider in my family is/was my __ because...
- If I could change myself I would like to be like [family member] because...
- There is no one in my family I want to be like because...
- In my family we are/were very close /not close at all because...
- My father was closest to me/to my __ because...
- My mother was closest to me/to my __ because...
- The most important person in my family was __ because...
- Children were considered as/treated as...

- My family was/was not divided into groups and the groups were... (list them)

- In describing myself I would say I am...

- When I drew the picture of my family I felt and drew myself as __ years old because...

- When I drew my family we were living in __ and the year was __

- List the people in your family of origin and current family (if you have one)

- In that list, name something you need in the next five years from each member in your family of origin...

- In that list, name something you want to do in the next five years for each member in your family of origin...

Look over the pictures your drew of God and your family. Do you see any resemblances? If so, list some of these resemblances in your notebook.

### PAYING ATTENTION TO SPIRITUAL NEEDS

Recall the case studies involving Jake and Marjorie. Their stories contained universal and ordinary human needs. These needs are both spiritual and material. Material needs might be obvious, but one purpose of theological dialogue is to meet and satisfy people's spiritual needs through spiritually satisfying conversation, reflection with others, prayer, insight from tradition, and other Christian rituals that offer the means for healing and wholeness as reminders of God's grace.

The following spiritual needs are a focal point for Theological Reflection because every human being has a spiritual need to:

- Celebrate

- Mark significant moments

- Bear witness to truths learned about life
- Tell their story
- Grieve and mourn
- Lament
- Connect with the past
- Make significant journeys
- Express themselves symbolically
- Seek purpose and meaning
- Ask ultimate questions
- Survive and flourish
- Experience longing and enjoy satisfaction
- Relax
- Play
- Cope with life circumstances
- Be seen
- Be heard
- Have a name
- Be part of a larger community
- Organize experience meaningfully
- Maintain human dignity

**Questions for Reflection**

When have you experienced these needs in your own life? How do you usually respond to your own needs? Write about a time when you found a particularly meaningful way to meet one of these spiritual needs. How do you think a group of people engaged in theological reflection could meet each other's spiritual needs effectively? List some of the ways.

---

**EXERCISE: SPEAKING WITH OTHERS**

Take the opportunity to find time with someone you trust. Give this person an example of a spiritual need you have that isn't being met. Give an example of a spiritual need that's currently being met for you.

---

**EXERCISE: SCENARIO**

Read the following scenario, and list Darren's spiritual needs. Given the reality of his spiritual needs, describe how you would console Darren?

---

DARREN

Darren grew up in a Christian home. He had two sisters. His parents were very involved in the local church. His father attended meetings most evenings. When Darren got his first bike, he asked his father to help him learn to ride it. He and his father were just going out the door, hand in hand, when a couple from the church stopped by. They wanted to talk. Darren's father let go of his hand and welcomed the couple with a friendly handshake. He invited them into the house.

Darren touched his father's hand and asked: "What about my bike?" He said it quietly, but it was loud enough for the couple to hear. His father told him to go to his room. Later that night he got all three children together and said that it was their Christian duty to help people in need. He was angrier than the children had ever seen him. He said that he never wanted one of his children to be so selfish again.

---

As you reflect on your response to Darren, what insights about family and faith can you add to your personal inventory?

# Notes

1. Claude Levi-Strauss, *Myth and Meaning* (London: Routledge, 2003), 7.

2. *Myth and Meaning*, 40.

3. *Myth and Meaning*, 40.

4. *Myth and Meaning*, 44.

5. *Myth and Meaning*, 36.

6. Karen Armstrong, *A Short History of Myth* (New York: Canongate, 2005), 4.

7. A. Berlin and M. Zvi Bretter, *The Jewish Study Bible* (Oxford: Oxford University Press, 2004), 2134.

8. *The Jewish Study Bible*, 9.

9. Some of these questions are derived from Ana-Maria Rizzuto's book *Birth of the Living God* and many of them are questions that Bellous and Sheffield have asked for many years.

CHAPTER 6

# SPIRITUAL TYPES THAT INFLUENCE
# THEOLOGICAL REFLECTION

I f we consider the role that myth plays in the ordinary stories we tell ourselves, based on our own personal experience, as well as on our family, culture or national stories, it's clear that even members of the same family will tell a different story about the world and what to expect from life. It's an obvious comment, perhaps, but, as a result, people involved in theological reflection will be quite different from one another. Because of those differences, theological conversations are an opportunity to gain insight from those who differ from us so we can develop a more holistic view of the Christian life. To that end, this chapter includes a description of four spiritual types that characterize Western and Eastern Christianity down through the centuries. These spiritual types will differ within our families of origin as well.

Getting a sense of these different types can explain a great deal about disagreements and conflict if people have different interpretations of faith and Christian practice. Based on a book by Corinne Ware, Figures #3 and #4 organize the four types, pointing out what's important in each one.[1] Ware's purpose in providing this map was to show that, while people have preferences, Christians develop in these four areas if they wish to be whole. In conversation with other believers, we have an opportunity to identify these differences in the way we communicate. In line with the previous chapter, the diagrams provide another global perspective on the range of options within Christianity.

Up to now theological reflection is described as a conversation we have with God, other people and ourselves in which we try to get clear about how we think, act and believe when dealing with a destabilizing situation. Conversation may go off the rails and never become dialogue if people see things so differently they can't interpret the language and narrative used by others who are part of the conversation. We can get back on track during these conversations by relying on insight from the four spiritual types, once we recognize them. That insight can adjust the way we communicate in order to connect with those who see Christianity differently.

## FIGURE #3 FOUR SPIRITUAL TYPES

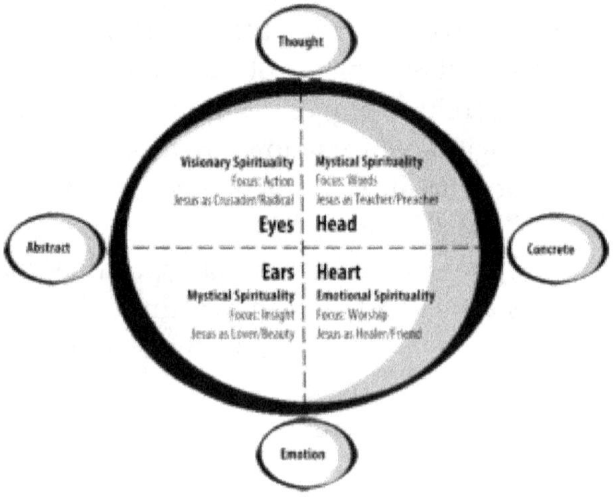

Thought

Visionary Spirituality | Mystical Spirituality
Focus: Action | Focus: Words
Jesus as Crusader/Radical | Jesus as Teacher/Preacher

**Eyes | Head**

Abstract

Concrete

**Ears | Heart**

Mystical Spirituality | Emotional Spirituality
Focus: Insight | Focus: Worship
Jesus as Lover/Beauty | Jesus as Healer/Friend

Emotion

*based on Corinne Ware, Discover Your Spiritual Type. (Lanham, MD: Rowman & Littlefield, 1995.)*

Notice that Figure #4 divides the four types into two aspects of spiritual experience. The types divide into two differently oriented sub-cultures, which are described by the predominance of silence on the one side and talk on the other. Some religious cultures can be described by this primary difference: those that tend to use talk as a way to express faith experience and those that tend to rely on silence as a way to express faith experience. This fundamental difference between religious expressions can be very difficult to bridge unless we listen carefully to what others are saying or not saying.

- Sound: word, music, talk, singing, confessing, witnessing, concrete representation

- Silence: thought, sight, hearing, receiving, listening, imagining, acting, idealization

As we examine the four spiritual types from this perspective, note that some Christian groups create a talking culture, while others constitute a silent culture.

**FIGURE #4 TWO DIMENSIONS OF THE FOUR SPIRITUAL TYPES**

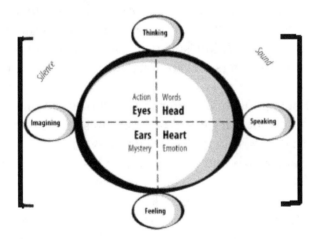

In a conversation, if one person is mystical and image oriented (from the perspective of silence) and the other is cognitive and word oriented (from the perspective of talk) it's easy to misunderstand and offend each other. If we pay attention to patterns created by these differences and decode the other person's meaning in terms of them, dialogical theological conversations can come about. The description of four spiritual types is a useful map for working toward dialogue if theological conversations begin running into trouble.

The next section includes a description of four spiritual types, one or two of which may be typical of you. As you read these descriptions, reflect on theological conversations that haven't gone well for you. Do these descriptions add any insight to what went wrong?

## INTELLECTUAL SPIRITUALITY

*(Speculative, Kataphatic, Cognitive; God as revealed in words)*

Those who look at Christianity from this point of view take a thoughtful, cognitive approach to spiritual experience based on the significance of words. The focus is primarily verbal: to get the right words right. Words and accuracy are important; becoming more correct about the words of the faith is perceived as a means of spiritual transformation. Maturing faith becomes more and more reflective about the Biblical text and other texts as well. Within this type, if words are accurate, then faith is thought of as well grounded. In addition, spiritual transformation is expressed through increased personal understanding. Scripture is highly valued.

Gifted people of this type produce scholarship and rigorous theological commentary based on a careful search of the content of the faith. Propositional knowledge is valued because it lays out important words and puts them in right relationship to one another. The spoken word is central so there is a focus on preaching and proclamation. Skills of rational argument are employed to persuade unbelievers of the veracity of the faith. Those who are at home in this type view faith in concrete terms. *Kataphatic* refers to affirmation so there is a tendency to think of God as revealed, knowable and concretely available. God is represented anthropomorphically. This type prizes what can be seen, touched, and vividly imagined. Its focus is God the Father. Right living and reliance on ethical imperatives are of great significance.

Extreme and distorted forms of head spirituality degenerate

into rationalism (a tendency to privilege thinking over feeling, doing and observing), also into cognitivism and conceptual moralism, in which all that matters is having the right idea, word or meaning and practising in the right way by carrying out rituals repeatedly with precision (orthopraxy). A moralizing tone points out that everyone who doesn't concur in word and deed is incorrect. In its extreme form, emotion isn't relevant to truth and is so unreliable that extreme individuals fail to recognize that thinking and feeling work together in mental activity. (It a mistake to think brains separate out thinking and feeling.) Yet if individuals of this type make a contribution out of their intellectual wealth, that contribution is key to the development of religious understanding.

## EMOTIONAL SPIRITUALITY

*(Affective, Kataphatic, Heartfelt; Expressive; God as revealed in experience)*

Often in reaction to the extremes of the first type, with heart spirituality, emotion is central. Like head spirituality, a concrete expression of God is highly prized. Music and oral witness play central roles. In this type, emotion and concrete representation are key to the life of faith. This type of faith expression values what's deeply felt as good in itself and, far from being an indolent substitute for scholarship, emotional intelligence entails more, not less, hard work. With an emotion focus, it's the hard work of holy living and a free expression of feeling, embodied as well as oral, which initiates and sustains spiritual maturity. God is here, now, immanent, relational. Christ is the satisfying lover of the soul. In contrast to type one, intellectualism is suspect. Evangelism matters, but rather than rational arguments, this type focuses on flashes of insight or words of knowledge that are got directly from God. The transformation goal within this type is personal renewal.

Extreme forms of type two are Pietism (a movement promoting personal religious devotion to God as Savior), Enthusiasm and Emotionalism. Tension between head and heart types were typical of the eighteenth century. For example, Kant abhorred what he called Enthusiasm and insisted on pure reason as a compass for thinking as a rational human being. The divide between head and heart is a fulcrum of modernity. To their discredit, extreme forms of heart spirituality fail to notice how unresolved pain, suffering and loss motivate their spiritual agenda. This personality can be driven by under-analyzed emotion. Its leaders may refuse to be held accountable for undue influence on followers. Leadership may be moved by spiritual hunches if hard emotional work isn't done. Heart spirituality is highly contagious but religious leaders of this type can draw followers toward harm.

If extreme forms of head spirituality tend to isolate adherents due to an abrasive demand for correctness, extreme forms of heart spirituality tend to unite disenchanted followers under common emotional causes that may persist regardless of their enduring worth. Yet twentieth century resources from type two awakened the Church in North America, and the West generally, to the Holy Spirit. Communal celebrations of worship music revitalized church experience. Christianity is indebted to gifted individuals of this type for renewing the heart of faith and practice.

To compare them, if preaching is a focus for the first, type two groups emphasize worship. It's possible to see the North American worship wars of the last few decades as a large-scale shift from type one to type two practices.

In terms of theological reflection, if people from each type try to converse about their beliefs, practices and understanding of scripture, it's easy to see how their conversation could erupt in conflict. A telltale sign you're talking to someone from a different type is the discomfort you feel around the way they describe worship or the anger or insult you feel because you sense they're implying you aren't as good a Christian as they are. For example, you may get the sense that you're not using the right words in the right way (Orthodoxy in type one) or not using appropriate feelings to the right degree (Orthopathy in type two).

If you pause and perceive the dissonance in your

conversation you can adapt the way you're speaking to employ words, images, feelings or to suggest action until mutual trust is built up. Then you're free to explain your own perspectives in a friendly manner. Affirm what might be the other person's emphasis first before you advocate for your own. You can begin to affirm them by inquiring into what matters most to them. It's ideal for a Christian believer to value the strengths of all four types so as to incorporate a reasonable balance among them. In balancing them, people tend not to exaggerate any one type to its extreme.

## MYSTICAL SPIRITUALITY

*(Apophatic, Mystery; Impressive; God revealed Inwardly; Imagined, as Image during Ritual)*

For both head and heart personalities, the need and freedom to express one's way of being Christian is paramount so that both of these dispositions tend to create a talking culture if they dominate a religious community. The other two spiritual personalities are unified by a disposition born of silence that withdraws from expressing in words the profound spiritual meanings and passions of people in quadrants three and four. Head and heart spiritualities are demonstrative and verbal; the third is passive, receptive and waits to hear God speak rather than to speak for God.

The third personality is the mystic. The theological term *Apophatic* implies negation and refers to conceiving of God in non-concretized ways, as mystery. Mystery, by definition, is elusive, more sensed than spoken. Mystery is above being captured in words, unavailable for complete revelation this side of heaven. In quadrant three, explaining spiritual experience isn't attractive; if one tries, something precious is lost. Mystic spirituality combines emotion, solitude, and the music of the spheres. There tends to be a focus on the beauty of creation, on the beauty of God's own self, conveyed from Heart to heart. The primary body metaphor is hearing and its emphasis is on perception of the Unseen. The transformational goal is union with God through the Holy Spirit. The imagination is nourished by manifestations of God's presence. Those with this personality provide the Christian community with devotional works that push the boundaries of spiritual experience.

Extreme forms of this type draw one toward Reclusivity and Quietism (a group that waits on God and practices the abandonment of self to God). Practitioners withdraw from trying to express outwardly what's perceived inwardly. Inexpressible aspects dominate the need to communicate orally. Words aren't available; communion with other ordinary people is abandoned. Gnosticism, an extreme form of inward knowing, denies value to the material world and abuses the body through ascetic practice.

Some experienced monks of the Eastern Christian tradition fell into this extreme. Yet without the mystical warmth that deepens and broadens spiritual experience, we're left with cold, hard ideas that don't sustain us in the crises of life and don't explain strange, supernatural encounters human beings have, even those who say they don't believe in God. Gifted people in this quadrant can experience God's presence in a sunrise or a fog settling quietly down to the earth — an experience that satisfies and sustains their spiritual need to hear God and know union with God. They remind us that God is more than human.

### VISIONARY SPIRITUALITY

*(Speculative, Apophatic, Concrete; Demonstrated; God revealed in and as Action)*

An inability to express itself fully in words links type three with type four spirituality. In type four, it's what one does, not what one says, which is central. Type four speculative and concrete aspects drive an individual to attempt to change the world, rather than only pray for it, as a mystic might do. If the transformational goal for the third type is union with God, the goal for type four is to change conditions in the world that cause harm. The focus is on seeing justice done. People of this type are single-minded, passionate, observant, impatient, thought-provoking prophets.

They're driven by concrete conditions in the world to protest injustice and to eradicate it. They're motivated by a union with the world's deepest needs; meeting them effectively is an unswerving mission. If a mystic spirituality is lived out in quietness and isolation, this spiritual type is moved by an isolating need to save the world single-handedly, often without the help of others who are judged to be too blind to see what needs to be done or too cowardly to accomplish it.

With this type, *Encratism* is an early, extreme form (an early Christian sect that abstained from meat, wine and marriage). Another extreme is practical moralism that alienates other people at the same time that it calls them to join in world-saving mission. Without the skill of words, of persuasion, this type can't easily draw others toward the forceful call on their lives. The world must be saved at all cost. There's no time to talk; action alone justifies one's claim to be a faithful follower of the radical Jesus.

Even its moderate exercise tends to alienate others since there's little that modifies type four passion. Alienating others is in part caused by the inability to articulate what needs to be done and give reasons for doing it. Even moderates are ruled by impatience. This type may ridicule and insult others who appear to be less committed. It can be activism for its own sake, harshly judging others who fail to see the urgency of needs or act quickly enough to meet them. Yet if this type is moderated by compassion (their own or another person's for them) and infused with humility, one life can change the world in God's name.

In summary, and as mentioned earlier, we have been defining spirituality as a sense of felt connection. This definition is not inharmonious with Ware's work. She builds spirituality on a concept of connection. To her spiritual sensibility is a connection to God and refers to the intentional attentiveness of various practices and styles of prayer. As an example, each type will have a way of praying that focuses on its central attributes. In addition, there are distinct differences between the types regarding their attitudes about the world as a whole, their ways of conceiving of God, their aspirations for relating to God, others and self through private as well as public means. For Ware, spiritual work is moved by values about how to live a worthy life. It's a response to our ultimate concerns. As you consider differences among spiritual types and their distinct contributions to Christianity, are there insights from this analysis that might apply to Jake or Marjorie as a way to explain situations they seem to have them trapped? Are there blind spots in each type that's been identified in this chapter that could explain some of what's gone wrong for Marjorie or Jake?

At this point, please reread their stories. Compare them with the following diagrams. See if there are generative themes, universal needs or blind spots that emerge from their spiritual personalities, as you might guess them to be, which help to articulate their present situation in a way that might make a good future more plausible for them. How would understanding their spiritual types help you converse with them effectively? Can you think of people in your own ministry that make no sense to you but may have a different spiritual type than you? How might reflecting on the four types help you understand some of the differences between these people and you up to this point?

---

**EXERCISE: SIMILARITIES AND DIFFERENCES**

It's useful to compare personal spiritual types with congregational types. Spend time thinking about the four quadrants. Consider the dominant personality of your congregation. As you reflect on your own and their spiritual types, answer the following questions. Read the descriptions carefully and try to become more observant of when you or other people are coming from a different quadrant.

Ask yourself:

- Is your personality similar or different from your congregation's type?

- If they're similar, you may feel you fit; if different, you may feel you don't fit.

- If you don't fit, and you try to lead theological reflection, what will happen?

- If others in the congregation differ from you, and don't fit, what will happen as you lead theological reflection?

- How can theological reflection encompass all four ways for being Christian?

- What do you need to learn to lead theological reflection with others who are different from you?

Assessing the spiritual types offers the following benefits:

- Helps people self-identify so as to find explanatory frameworks for self-understanding

- Enables people to understand each other so they don't personalize their differences

- Informs leaders of the differences that are characteristic of the four types

- Paints the broadest picture for personality so that theological reflection creates and encourages the development of all these ways of being spiritual and theological

- Encourages people to work at all these ways of knowing and loving God to become more like Christ, who expressed all four styles in his ministry on earth

- Offers moderating effects on a spiritual excess of pursuing only one way to be Christian, especially in churches and denominations

If the aim of being inclusive of different Christian ways of experiencing God and being faithful to God are taken seriously, worship, education, theological reflection and Christian practice will include the following emphases:

- The scholarly discipline of learning, understanding and applying the meaning of words
- The hard work of emotional learning through feeling, music, movement, and the arts
- The communal and personal participation in meaningful rituals will strengthen people's resolve to live a life of faith
- The act of carrying out plans that make the world better and more just will be brought into theological reflection, so that it becomes theological praxis

Perhaps you wonder if self-observation is really a good thing. What if you find something in your own heart that frightens or frustrates you? In this chapter, there's an opportunity to become more self-aware. Yet healthy self-observation is not self-absorption. Just as observing your own and other people's spirituality types helps to remember that a focus on word, emotion, image and action must be included in theological reflection, healthy reflection is never self-focused concern for our own well-being at the expense of other people. Observing ourselves isn't the same as being concerned only with ourselves; it mustn't be allowed to lead to spiritual and emotional isolation. Observing ourselves has to do with noticing what's in our own hearts and paying attention to the movement of our own souls as we move closer in friendship with God.

Collaborative theological reflection is an antidote to living the Christian life in isolation, a primary problem both Jake and Marjorie haven't faced in an educationally transformative manner. If you want to be helpful to people such as Jake and Marjorie, learning how to provide your own true and best reasons for how and why you read scripture the way you do is a good start. In the next exercise, spend one hour to work through an Expanded *Lectio Divina*. This form adds *Sapientia*, engaged knowledge that's infused with trust and healing. Hopefully, this exercise offers new insight into God's love for you and God's presence with you.

---

**EXERCISE: AN EXPANDED LECTIO DIVINA**

This adapted format for *Lectio Divina* helps to identify blind spots as we think, speak and act. Blind spots get in the way of seeing clearly as we dialogue with ourselves internally, with God who is Wholly Other or with believers whose experience and perceptions of the faith differ from ours. Having blind spots doesn't mean there's something wrong with us. Everyone has them. But it's important to recognize blind spots. Sometimes, they indicate that we're using unhealthy reason to misguide ourselves about faith and what it's like to follow Jesus.

As mentioned, an expanded *Lectio Divina* includes a way of knowing called Sapientia and its use clarifies relationships between faith and reason. Clarifying those relationships is a means for working more effectively to develop a capacity for personal and collaborative inquiry. As has already been stated, people learn through self-observation in conversation. Growth comes as that self-observation nurtures the human spirit and allows us to hear God, other people and ourselves.

Please consider the invitation to engage in the revised plan for *Lectio Divina*. *Sapientia* adds to sacred reading a form of reasoning that has three characteristics: knowledge is assumed, reason is employed and trust is essential. The role of trust is crucial. *Sapientia* makes it possible to distinguish between healthy and unhealthy reason. Cynicism, or the voice of the skeptic, e.g., Satan in the Zechariah passage, doesn't function in *Sapientia*. This is because, unlike relentless skepticism that annihilates any potential for trust to develop, *Sapientia* is founded on trust and builds trust. Yet healthy reason is still employed.

Healthy reason is a studied way to make good judgments about experience. Including reason in this exercise encourages those engaged in reflection to explore God's nature, human experience and cultural influences, by bringing scripture and tradition to bear on issues in a focused manner; in particular, by becoming aware of one's own true and best reasons for why we experience God as we do. Reason is essentially the developed capacity to be a good judge of experience—sense experience (using directly observable data) and lived experience (worldview) and helps us learn from both. As outlined in an earlier chapter, reason is a peculiarly stubborn effort to get clear about something. To build that stubborn effort on the basis of trust is as reasonable as it is to build on a foundation of skepticism—except for the fact that building reason on skepticism means never coming to a settled position on the inquiry. Skepticism never stops long enough to rest or relax. It will never meet the spiritual needs everyone has to relax into answers to major life concerns.

People have the capacity to trust and relax into meanings made from experience from childhood. This is the basis for making sense of life, which isn't the same as being right about world. Rather, we compile a meaningful worldview that allows us to function in the world. Having meaning and being right aren't the same but we come to think they are. What else would people assume before it occurs to them that they can begin to reflect on that worldview?

Consider the data you accumulated by answering questions in the previous chapter that helped to identify aspects of the worldview you formed from an early age, based on your personal experience. A worldview becomes our comfort zone. Healthy reason works with worldviews as well as the cultural patterns and God concepts that shape personal and communal belief and practice. In addition, healthy reason is held accountable by referring to directly observable data, to use Farber Robinson's expression.

In effective theological reflection, reason is employed but not as a stand-alone. It leads us to think through worldviews that are already there (i.e., knowledge is assumed) but it isn't in charge of the outcome, i.e., the product produced. Rather, reason is a servant. The expanded *Lectio Divina* isn't better than the traditional one. They differ and can be used for different purposes. The expanded approach offers a way for reason to be devotional. It's a solid foundation on which to build collaborative theological reflection because it allows people to see some of their true and best reasons for thinking and believing as they do. With the expanded model, participants gain access to these reasons and can offer them to others in conversation.

The expanded model takes longer than the historical practice and requires having some resources on hand. For example, a dictionary, more than one translation or version of the passage and a Bible Dictionary are needed. In addition, a Theological Word Book of the Bible is useful. If you use Greek, you'll want to have these resources handy as well. This isn't a time to read other people's books on the passage. Use only basic resources to get closer to the meaning of the words in the text itself. This isn't a time for study in the usual sense. So often we get data so we can transfer it to an assignment, lecture, sermon, essay, book or presentation. This is a time to unpack what you think as you reflect on a passage and come up with some sense of why you might think it, with help from the Holy Spirit.

This emphasis is important. You aren't being invited into meditative practice in order to get something for other people. You're entering into sacred reading to hear your own heart! You will use what you gain later on, but that's not the point now. You'll miss out if you focus on secondary assignments and the needs of other people during this practice. This time is for you and God to converse together. Don't let other issues intrude into time set aside for the lover of your soul. In what follows, there are four elements of *Lectio Divina* and an opportunity to use *Sapientia*, which guides the use of reason. May the expanded practice enrich your life and persuade you of how much you are loved by God.

*Lectio* (Using the senses to perceive – the focus is on sensing)

Read the passage of scripture. Sacred reading begins by listening to the words you're looking at on the page. Read slowly enough to allow them to sink in, quickly enough to keep from being distracted. The ancients attributed eagerness to this first reading: there's something here you want to sense. It's reverential reading. As you focus on the text, and because you have set aside time to be with God, there may be tears as you read. Let them come. Deep emotion was closely connected with *Lectio Divina*. Don't try to understand why you weep at this reading; let emotion enrich your devotional encounter with these words.

Write notes on all the insights that come to you and that stand out to you...


You're listening for the voice of God — for a still, small voice that beckons to you from the text. Remember to breathe freely, sitting with a relaxed but not slumped posture. Be attentive to the atmosphere of the passage be fully present. Imagine what it would be like to be there: picture the landscape, the people, the immediate surroundings, the climate. Sit quietly. Think about those involved in the passage. What do you learn about them from the story? Use as many senses as possible to engage the story and to make it come alive for you.

Is there anyone who's something like you in this passage? This isn't a time to think about what the text means but what you sense in it. You're not responsible right now for bringing this text to anyone else. This time is for you alone. Listen for God as you read. To hear God speak, we must be silent. Quiet yourself. Listen for a word, phrase, image, sensation that stands out. Reverential reading is harder for some than for others. Relax. See what happens.

*Meditatio* (Using cognition to ruminate – the focus is on remembering)

Read the passage again, this time ask yourself "Why?" Consider the meaning and significance of the passage. This is a time for thinking in a certain sense that's more like ruminating or chewing on what you have found. Why were those particular words or images included? Why was it written in this way? What is being taught? If you are having difficulty finding meaning for the passage, try pretending to be a character you can identify with, or all the characters. What do you already know about this sort of person? How does that knowledge inform your reading? In this section your goal is to understand the meaning of the passage based on what you know and what you've experienced. Thinking involves the past: we think about what we already know. Try to gather your thoughts from past experience, past associations.

What do you know about this text? What do you wonder about it? Does it remind you of something? How is one phrase, image or idea linked to another? Does any word or image remind you of another passage of scripture? Don't look it up as yet, just try to remember. What are your questions? Write them down. What's the main point or lesson that you can take away from the text? What's it about? Take some of your ideas and ponder them, as Mary did, after Christ was born and angels and shepherds came to celebrate his birth. (Luke 2:19)

Write notes on all the insight that comes to you and what stands out to you...

Memorize an aspect of the passage or the whole of it. Let it sink in. Let the words touch and affect you at a deep level so that what you read is personal. Welcome God's words into your life. Allow these signs (black marks on a page) to be living words, and a message from God in which God is present. It's at this point that we might say: Oh I see! I get it! That's what it's about. Focus on what you can add to words of scripture that you've already memorized.

*Sapientia* (Using reason to rethink – the focus is on recognizing)

At this point, read the passage again and refocus on words, phrases, events, metaphors that stood out to you, some of which you memorized. In your earlier readings, you attended to meanings you already had for these words. You selected what mattered by considering what you already knew or have experienced. That is, you thought of the past and how it influences your present interpretation of the passage. It was important to write down these insights in the first two parts of the practice in order to have a written record of what you emphasized in these readings.

Now, focus on the story you're telling yourself about the way you read this scripture. By telling yourself and God the story that underlies why you read the passage the way you do, you become more aware of what currently moves your thought and emotion. To organize the meaning you attach to the text, refer to the section on Theological Reflection as Representation. Using a pattern that works for you, organize your meaning for the text by describing the whole picture in words and images that convey what's central to the meaning of the passage. Write down and draw why you think of these words, images, events as you do. Does a person or memory present itself as you represent the meaning of the passage? What comes to mind? Engage in this exercise prayerfully.

It's very important not to jump ahead to the *Sapientia* phase while you're meditating on your second reading. If you jump ahead and shortcut meditation, the reasoning part of the process won't provide all the results you want; you'll reduce the practice to mere study, which has its own value but isn't what you want to accomplish in this expanded form of sacred reading.

The meaning of the word *Sapientia* helps to understand what you attempt at this point. There are three parts to the process based on the word's meaning: knowledge, reason and trust. In your earlier two readings you identified and recorded your knowledge. Consider the Zechariah 3:1-7 passage and put yourself into a frame of mind that enjoys certainty that God loves you. God is Friendly. Trusting God depends on his promise of love, on

Jesus' life, death and resurrection, not only on your strength to work at it. Give yourself some time to rest in the love of God. Consider the scripture from 2 Corinthians 3:18ff as you reflect on God's love.

> And we, who with unveiled faces all [contemplate] the Lord's glory, are being transformed into his likeness with ever-increasing glory, which comes from the Lord, who is the Spirit... Therefore, since through God's mercy we have this ministry, we do not lose heart....For God, who said, "Let light shine out of darkness," made his light shine in our hearts to give us the light of the knowledge of the glory of God in the face of Christ. But we have this treasure in jars of clay to show that this all-surpassing power is from God and not from us... It is written: "I believed; therefore I have spoken." With that same spirit of faith we also believe and therefore speak, because we know that the one who raised the Lord Jesus from the dead will also raise us with Jesus and present us with you in his presence.
>
> All this is for your benefit, so that the grace that is reaching more and more people may cause thanksgiving to overflow to the glory of God. Therefore we do not lose heart. Though outwardly we are wasting away, yet inwardly we are being renewed day by day. For our light and momentary troubles are achieving for us an eternal glory that far outweighs them all. So we fix our eyes not on what is seen, but on what is unseen. For what is seen is temporary, but what is unseen is eternal.

After considering that God is love, it's time to give yourself the true and best reasons you have for your understanding of the passage of scripture that you chose or was given to you for sacred reading. To reason is to question, call to account or hold argument (dialogue) in order to influence conduct or opinion.

To reason is to think in a connected, sensible or logical manner in order to form conclusions. Recall that you're to distinguish healthy from unhealthy reason. Reason is misused if we employ the following ways of talking and thinking; if we

- Belittle ourselves, our experiences, or our reasons for belief and thought

- Analyze them by giving simple reasons that effectively blow them off

- Blame someone else or focus on someone else's part in why we think/act as we do

- Suppress our thoughts and beliefs by 'gritting our teeth and bearing it'

- Lecture ourselves about how stupid we are to see things this way
- Drown in the feelings attached to the reasons for our belief, thought or actions

Reason is misused if we come to think our concerns aren't serious or signify we're worthless, hopeless and alone.

What we understand about reason is important. Reason has more than one meaning. It refers to a structured sequence of ideas, whose unity has as its purpose to uncover or establish what's true and good. Reason also refers to the why of my actions and thought, e.g., I give you my reason for doing or thinking something. Reason is employed in both senses in what follows. Give reasons for thinking as you do about the passage. Your whole story about it will have a coherent structure that aims at finding its truth and goodness. The story you tell will have reasons in the first sense, a plot and a dramatic line that you may draw using non-linguistic representation.

To begin then, there must be a reason to create the story you tell about this passage, i.e., your interpretation of it. What's there in it that triggers your interest? It may be something novel, unexpected, confusing or troubling. A reason is a spark that ignites your interest in a passage. The story you tell yourself (and God) depends on implicit assumptions about how the world works and what can normally be expected from life. You may recognize some of what you gathered in the section on personal worldview. Your story also has a plot; it contains who, why, what, when and where of your interpretation of the passage. The plot makes the elements of your story cohere. Finally, your story has a line of dramatic tension that carries the action toward the future. What's the outcome of the way you interpret this passage? Where is it taking you? Toward what action is your story drawing you? The non-linguistic representation of the story will give you the clearest idea of its dramatic line.

Once you have an ordered interpretation of the passage and can say why you think you see it this way, by naming your associations with it based on personal experience, move on to the next step. The aim of *Sapientia* in sacred reading is to take what you already think about the passage (and your reasons for thinking it) and hold them up to what you learn by using the resources at your disposal. In this phase you are reasoning with yourself. You hold your own thinking accountable based on a wider understanding of the passage. This learning is personal. You're trying to get a better sense of why you think the way you do and to accept an opportunity for growth in understanding.

It's personal in another sense also. You're trying to let God love you more. Suppose the passage triggers an image of the expression on God's face. If God were right beside you, what would that expression look like? The Bible says that God is love. Would the look on God's face be loving as God gazes at you? Why is that? Suppose you read a passage about someone who lacks faith. And in reflecting on it, you're aware of a feeling of reluctance to give yourself fully to God as a person of faith. What is that feeling like? What are your reasons for feeling this way? Does an event in your life appear and seem to be important? How does trusting that God is love help you imagine yourself as a person with potential to be faithful?

At this point, allow yourself to recognize differences between what scripture promises or declares and what your story conveys. Record these differences. Construct the logic of scripture and set it beside the logic of your own thought. Tell the truth. This is all you're required to do at this point. You'll have two sets of data: your current reasons and story and your research from carefully re-reading the passage using the resources you brought. Even if there is only one small difference, pay attention to it and move to the *Oratio* stage.

*Oratio* (Using emotion to respond – the focus is on feeling)

Set the two ways of looking at the passage in front of you and invite feeling and thinking about them to be united in prayer. *Oratio* is a way into prayer through meditative reading "with purity of heart and potentially tears." Let the continual meditation penetrate your heart and form it according to promises of God you're receiving through scripture. As you read the passage again, talk to God. Consider how the passage affects you emotionally, particularly with respect to differences between what you were thinking initially and what you're being challenged to consider. Don't hurry.

What are you feeling? There are no incorrect feelings. As you pray, tell God your feelings. Especially be focused on feeling that's based on differences between what you've always thought and what you're being challenged to consider. This is emotional work and it's very hard sometimes.

Becoming astute about your own emotion has to do with sensing what you feel to see how it affects thought and action. There are patterns to the way you feel. These patterns may become more evident as you continue to read this book. There's an underlying pattern in the passage that you've focused on. If it differs from the pattern in your worldview, this is the time to bring these differences to God, whether they're slight or significant. Suppose the passage invites you to consider that God is generous, yet your worldview got its start in emotional, relational poverty. Take this disparity and lay it at the foot of Christ's cross.

Let your feelings open up to the differences in your understanding of the passage. Only rarely are people really good at easily naming their feelings. If you're typically someone who shuts down feelings, recall your posture and your breathing. Regain a comfortable position and breathe. Perhaps you might lay your hands on your knees or in your lap in an open gesture to signal you want to understand yourself, as God understands you, because of what this passage touches in you.

To do this emotional work you need help from the Holy Spirit. Let the Spirit remind you of Jesus' life so you can be more comfortable doing the spiritual and emotional work of crying out to God. You want to be drawn closer to the heart of God. You want to realize what it means to be God's friend when Jesus says to his disciples that he no longer calls them servants, he calls them friends. (John 15:15) Offer what's on your heart to God so that God, who is the lover of your soul, can gaze on that offering. In this act, what we know about God is touched compassionately by what God knows about us and by the Good that God wants for our lives. If you don't feel anything, or anything deeply, tell that to God and sit quietly for a few minutes.

*Contemplatio* (Using intuition to internalize – the focus is on appropriating)

This final reading of the text encourages contemplation. Contemplation requires us to focus on an inner world. Now is the time to consider more fully the previous four activities and internalize them. Breathe. Contemplation involves nothing more than sitting quietly to listen and receive. First concentrate on breathing. Is it natural? Is your posture comfortable but not slouched? Focus on what your heart is telling you. Notice feelings and thoughts and return to a state of openness and expectation. You may be anxious, bored or frustrated: simply tell God what you're feeling, make no excuses, but ask for help. You may close your eyes. If you find you don't receive any insight, return to the words of scripture. To contemplate, you allow yourself to enter into quiet, centering peacefulness. Christians have described the practice as attentiveness,* which means giving full, complete, uncluttered attention to something. That's all you're being asked to do.

It's hard to contemplate if life is cluttered by duties, thoughts or people. Tell yourself that right now is not the time for fretting over these issues. Tell yourself that right now you can solve none of the problems that cause you trouble. God offers you undivided attention now and will be with you later as you try, with renewed strength and wisdom, to tackle problems and opportunities when the time is right to pay attention to them.

So much of the time people say to us: Don't just stand or sit there, do something! Now you can say to yourself: Don't just do something, sit here! Breathe comfortably and deeply. Remember that *Lectio Divina* is sacred reading for your personal spiritual benefit. If you let God in now, you will be able later to give other people and other projects the undivided attention that they need, and you will better at it. You will gain new insight about being attentive to others if you give full attention to God now.

At this point, assimilate words you've been reading and considering. Let God speak. Hear God's encouragement. Lift these differences up to the Lord and let God have a look at them. Allow the compassion that God offers you to grow in your heart so you gain compassion for yourself. After some time, end your meditation.

In summary, what are some of your observations about the difference in your experience of the first and the second versions of *Lectio Divina*? Name some of the patterns you identify in yourself that rely on unhealthy reason. What's one change you would like to make in how you speak to yourself? What's one change you would like to make in how you speak about and with other people? Name a change you would like to make in the way you think about God.

**Questions for Reflection**

There are elements of this exercise that help to understand Jake and Marjorie. Can you go back to their stories and consider them in light of insights from the exercises in this chapter? As you think again on Jake and Marjorie,

- Consider their relationship between the human spirit and the Holy Spirit.

- How would you describe their worldviews?

- What concepts of God have they acquired/constructed, do you think?

- What's the main story that Jake and Marjorie tell themselves about God?

- What common spiritual needs do you think Jake and Marjorie have?

- Try to guess at Jake and Marjorie's spiritual types

- How might knowing their spiritual type help them in their spiritual pilgrimage?

- How might the discipline of *Lectio Divina* impact these two people?

- How are you reading their stories now?

- Is there anything new in what you think about their situations?

- What scriptural passages would you use to begin a theologically reflective conversation with Jake and Marjorie if you wanted to shift the conversation to genuine dialogue?

In Chapter One, there's a three-step process for theological reflection. The steps include establishing the situation, imagining/envisioning possibilities and then taking action. What new insights do you have about the situation, its possibilities and the best action for Jake and Marjorie?

If both of them would consider change, how might that change come about? Change comes about as something new is added to our understanding of the situation we find ourselves in. It also comes about as we add to or gain new support for reasons we use to explain our actions. Can you add anything to the generative themes and contradictions in Jake and Marjorie's stories? Can you add anything to your understanding of their blind spots? What can you say about your own blind spots? What passages of scripture come to mind when you think about Jake and Marjorie?

Remember that generative themes help us connect our stories with the scriptural Story. Once we identify a generative theme, we recall scripture that relates to it and bring it to our aid with help from the Holy Spirit. The whole point of theological reflection is to begin and end in scripture. The next chapter focuses on collaborative theological reflection. When we work well with others, we multiply the access to spiritual resources and increase the ability to relate compassionately to problems in ministry and troubles in the world. The following chapter contains more of the arts that enable theological reflection to become a dialogue that's characterized by collaboration.

# Notes

1. In her book, *Discovering your Spiritual Type* (Lanham, MD: Rowman and Littlefield, 1995), Corinne Ware developed four spiritual types based on Urban T. Holmes analyses, particularly in the introduction to *A History of Christian Spirituality: An analytical introduction* (Minneapolis: Seabury, 1980).

# PART III

# COLLABORATIVE THEOLOGICAL REFLECTION

CHAPTER 7

# COLLABORATIVE INQUIRY

hapter One includes three models for theological reflection and outlines a general process to use with all of them. Model #1 puts embedded theology at the centre of an inquiry and encourages people to reflect on that embedded theology and then begin to deliberate on the theological ideas that characterized their perspectives up to that point in time. Model #2 focuses on assumptions at the centre of the inquiry and encourages those who inquire into the issues to recognize and reconsider assumptions they've been operating on.

Both models have a critical incident at the core of their approach that has destabilized the inquirer. Embedded theological insights and previously held assumptions no longer provide sufficient support for the ongoing spiritual process of making theological meaning out of ordinary experience. Model #3 also has a critical incident at its centre and works in situations in which there are at least two plausible, biblically sound ways of considering what should be done. In Model #3, action taken must conform to core principles, namely: love for and obedience to God, critical thinking, love for others and proper self-regard.

The general process outlined in Chapter One includes three steps: establishing the situation, imagining/envisioning the possibilities and taking appropriate action. Chapters Two to Six help people understand these three steps by expanding on how to see the situation more fully and imagine/envision possibilities in a given critical incident more expansively. The support these chapters provide includes practices such as *Lectio Divina*,

Focusing, Artful Listening and an Expanded *Lectio Divina* that incorporates *Sapientia*.

In addition, there's an explanation of The Trajectory of Reason and Soulful Thinking. The Prodigal Son story serves as a case study for the process of change that's possible as faith in God matures. A key component of a maturing faith is self-observation and the practice of the Eastern Orthodox tradition explained as Guarding the Heart. The stories of Jake and Marjorie are also offered in order to probe a given situation to suggest the need for change to take place if maturity in Christ in the ultimate goal of theological reflection.

However, while collaborative theological reflection has been described in earlier chapters, up to this point the practices named above could be carried out individualistically (with the exception of Guarding the Heart since participants in the Niptic tradition are adamant that the practice ought not to be carried out apart from a faith community).

In Collaborative Theological Reflection Model #4, the subject or destabilizing concern is put at the centre of the inquiry, as it is with the others. But at the beginning of that process, the knowledge and insight that everyone brings to the situation is expressed so that everyone involved becomes aware of how the situation is viewed by each other person, based on their past experience. If someone can't connect with the situation, it's clearly stated by that person.

A central feature of collaboration is the manner in which everyone's insights are brought to the inquiry. In collaboration, everyone is invited to offer knowledge of and experience with the situation (or similar ones) before anyone has a chance to analyze it individually, imagine or propose a solution or way forward. The steps to collaborative theological reflection are outlined later in the book, but it's important to understand what separates collaboration from individualistic approaches. Due to the inclusion of everyone's initial sense of what the situation means, a collaborative model builds toward a community of learning, in which truth is discovered during the conversation rather than handed down from authority figures (educational, clerical or civil) or brought to the table by one person.

At its core, this difference arises because the knowledge that's brought to the situation isn't in a finished form that assumes authority over all other interpretations. A community of learning works together to solve a problem that everyone unpacks until they understand it. Truth emerges as a result of that process. Truth is a conversation.

A community of learning uncovers universal themes in the situation and does so from multiple perspectives on it. Everyone brings their reality (narrative) to the table. Those perspectives on reality live in individual interpretations and expectations of what the problem involves and how it might be addressed through the corporate use of scripture, tradition and experience, along with help from the Holy Spirit. Scriptures, tradition, reason and experience are explored together in order to elaborate on the situation so as to understand what's going on within it as fully as possible.

A community of learning practices the art of problem solving by talking together. As Christian sociologist and educator, Parker Palmer noted,

> The hallmark of the community of truth is not psychological intimacy or political civility or pragmatic accountability, though it does not exclude these virtues. This model of community reaches deeper, into ontology and epistemology—into assumptions about the nature of reality and how we know it—on which all education is built. The hallmark of the community of truth is in its claim that reality is a web of communal relationships, and we can know reality only by being in community with it.[1]

In healthy theological collaboration, a community of truth emerges. The following chapters of the book focus on collaborative theological reflection by presenting a series of situations that are built around the experience of a man named David. His experience is divided into three exercises that take him to different locations. David's experience develops into a community of learning which has the potential to form a community of truth.

A community of learning, or truth in Palmer's terms, is built on mutual respect. In the next section, there's an assessment of the habit of respecting others. Following that assessment, there's an examination of how worldviews form assumptions and expectations that ground the way people construct meaning. Next, there's a discussion of how destabilizing events create dissonance and explain the role that dissonance plays in moving people toward transformation. Following the discussion on dissonance and in order to understand the dynamics of mutual respect, the roles of ordinary practices like feeling, talking and listening, all of which help people build a shared narrative and the desired outcome of collaborative inquiry, are explored. At the end is a definition of collaborative reflection itself.

### COLLABORATIVE INQUIRY IN GENERAL TERMS

What's implied by collaborative inquiry and how does it differ from individualistic inquiry? As a Christian spiritual practice, theological reflection is a conversation with God, scripture and the Christian community, past and present that achieves collaborative integrity, or truth in Palmer's terms. To make this claim more clearly, two questions need to be asked: What do people know and know how to do when they turn theological reflection into collaborative inquiry? Also, how does collaboration work? When people work together collaboratively they engage with knowledge in a different way than is most often the case when they try to work things out on their own.

That is, believers may be given tools for personal devotion or Bible study. They may investigate scripture or tradition to improve their spiritual life or to improve someone else's by teaching them they've already learned. Packets of already learned knowledge are on offer in the conclusions drawn from this investigation. Already formed knowledge from historical sources such as early councils (e.g., Nicene, Constantinople, Chalcedon) or from major theological minds such as Augustine, Aquinas,

Luther or Calvin are some examples. This knowledge is useful, particularly as we reflect on the worldview we got when we were young.

Yet very often believers act as if they're working on a finished product. That overconfidence might be expressed by saying something that sounds like, "its ok. I already I know this and I know there's nothing more to know." Recall the role that dialogue plays in theological conversation. Dialogue is also present when mutual respect characterizes that conversation. Mutual respect expresses itself in openness. Yet believers may rarely be given tools that lead to genuine dialogue. The big difference between personal and collaborative inquiry is personal inquiry aims to solve a problem, while collaborative inquiry aims to find a problem that's unfinished, unsolved and confusing. Bible study groups are a close relation to collaborative inquiry but even they may be mediated or directed by leaders and a set of expectations that foreclose on genuine dialogical theological reflection. We often work with knowledge that's already gathered, organized and polished into a finished product or we see our task as producing that finished bit of knowledge that we then ask others to adopt.

Even when we come to theological reflection as a group, those presenting may bring a set of assumptions and expectations that aren't analyzed by the group as part of its reflective process. But a destabilizing event can't be presented in this way. It's an event that doesn't fit the story we tell ourselves about the world. Often it's an event in which two narratives about the world collide because their deep assumptions, their blind spots don't mesh or make sense to one another. It may also represent a rift between two people that doesn't make sense to either one of them.

Collaborative inquiry invites us to come with unfinished, partial knowledge so that the whole group comes to an idea of what they know, believe and are called on by God to do as they reflect together. It's grounded on communal knowledge applied to a disturbing event that remains unresolved for the one who's bringing it to the group. During the collaborative process, generative themes, blind spots and universal needs are linked with scripture.

Collaborative theological inquiry that leads to a conversation and genuine dialogue is always based on bringing a messy, difficult and conflicted situation to the table. In this way, it's difficult to bring such an issue to most church Board meetings due to the time and the attitudes that are necessary for it to become collaborative. Yet, this is precisely where this kind of work should be done so that ministry practices of local churches shift from being shaped by strong-willed individuals (even godly ones) or pragmatic principles that have more to do with money than with the Holy Spirit. Ministry develops through collaborative reflection on God's Word, will and ways.

Respect for others is an essential attitude in collaborative theological reflection. The next section focuses on being respectful of others as a basic skill for collaborative theological reflection.

---

### RESPECT FOR OTHERS SELF-ASSESSMENT GUIDE

*Starting with Scripture*

Luke 7: 36-50     Jesus Anointed by a Sinful Woman

Luke 8: 40-53     A Dead Girl and a Sick Woman

As we read about Jesus' life on earth, we see someone who treated every human being he met with respect. It's surprising that Jesus could have maintained his composure in a social setting in which a woman was weeping at his feet, wiping his feet with her hair and pouring perfume upon him, while he sat at table with a group of elite, first century men. It's surprising that Jesus could be met by a woman with a curse of bleeding on his way to see a man who was rich and important and grant both of them his gift of time, attentiveness and healing.

Christians can become leaders and forget the essential and simple practice of respect for others. Respect for other people is most easily expressed by listening to what others are saying. One of the best habits we can cultivate is to appreciate other people by attending fully to them. Think of a situation you were in during the last week. Consider one that left you feeling a bit uneasy or angry. As you reflect back on the situation, ask yourself the following questions.

How would you rate yourself on the following? (1 is low and 4 is high)

1 2 3 4   I listen to other people as they are speaking

1 2 3 4   I look at people as they speaking and wait until they finish

1 2 3 4   I ask questions of one who is speaking to better understand

1 2 3 4   I welcome ideas by asking clarifying questions

1 2 3 4   I welcome ideas by asking for more information

1 2 3 4   I interrupt because I already know what they will say

1 2 3 4   I listen for a few minutes, nod, then change the subject

1 2 3 4   I demonstrate attention

1 2 3 4   I express appreciation

1 2 3 4   I state my affirmation whenever I can

How did you score on respect for others? 34 is the highest possible score.

Describe as fully as you can, a situation in which you felt deeply attended to, appreciated and affirmed by someone else. What was happening? How were attentiveness, appreciation and affirmation communicated? What did you like best about this experience? What would you like other people to experience when they're with you? Identify one change you would like to make in the way you attend to other people.

## WORLDVIEWS AND COLLABORATION

An underlying idea throughout this book is a belief that human spirituality is a framework for making meaning from everyday life. As the human spirit develops through dimensions of experience (biology, sociology, neurology, culture and psychology), everyone forms a worldview by early adolescence. With the formation of this worldview, we're endowed with, and also construct, ways of seeing and hearing that are congruent with the narratives that populated our personal experience. It's these worldviews, formed as we're growing up, that we bring to the table during collaborative theological reflection. The purpose of this section is to elaborate on the role these worldviews play so that participants in collaborative theological reflection can become more aware of what's shaping their thoughts and responses to what's going on in a destabilizing event.

A worldview is like a pair of glasses we look through. It's composed of a variety of stories that define and explain the world as a whole. It's packed with embodied concepts: ideas rich with emotion, infused with 'body language' as well as concepts for many aspects of life, including God concepts. What are these embodied concepts like? Suppose we see someone gesture in a way that reminds us of a person we intensely feared; fear is triggered by the gesture. The person we're with has no idea of the history of that gesture for us. Or perhaps someone uses a tone of voice that reminds us of someone we love; a warm memory arises immediately.

Experience and memory build a way of looking at the world that produces expectations for how things will go in the future and how the whole world works generally and in specific instances. The whole effect of a worldview moves us to predict what we think a given person will probably do or say, whether or not we're actually aware of these predictions.

Based on these worldviews, people bring a set of expectations for what will happen to any new setting. They learn what an experience means in relation to their expectations. As people learn, they continue to make meaning as they did early in life. A heightened sense of curiosity in children represents the vast amount of learning that must take place for them to develop expectations about the world, themselves and other people. Once expectations are layered into a meaning system (worldview) we tend to be less curious about what might happen next. A worldview warehouses assumptions and expectations so that we come to believe we already know what will happen next. The role expectations play in learning is always present.

All learning is organizing experience. People look for patterns in what they experience so they can make sense of what's happening and what they think will happen. The human brain operates in the process of forming expectations and organizing learning and builds memory as a part of the whole enterprise. Surprises occur if what we expect doesn't happen.

FIGURE #5 ORGANIZING EXPERIENCE

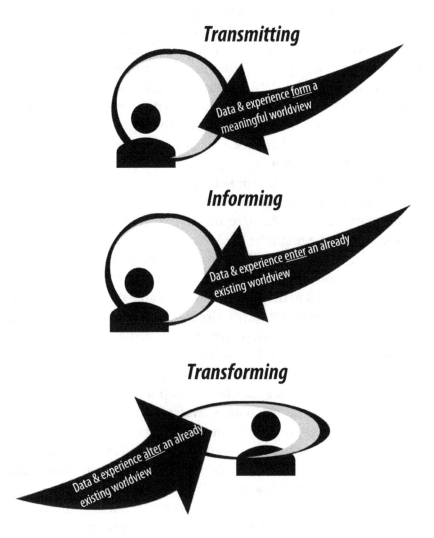

## Transmitting

Data & experience form a meaningful worldview

## Informing

Data & experience enter an already existing worldview

## Transforming

Data & experience alter an already existing worldview

For example, Jesus engaged in spiritual conversation of the sort we want to explore. He talked with Nicodemus, a Samaritan woman and Peter, to name a few. In these encounters, we can identify how worldviews function. Nicodemus came to Jesus with a vague question, not really a question, but it was personally important, even if it seemed like a test. In response, Jesus raised the issue of being born again. Nicodemus reacted with incredulity. They weren't on the same page about how faith works but the conversation opened up the possibility for a Jewish religious ruler to realize there might be something missing in his worldview. We aren't told the outcome of the conversation in this passage (John 3: 1-21) but Nicodemus offered support for Jesus later on (John 7:50) and came to get the body after the crucifixion (John 19:39). During their initial conversation, something happened to spark an intimate connection between them, which Nicodemus followed up later at considerable personal risk. This happened because conversing with Jesus impacted his worldview.

With the Samaritan woman, Jesus initiated a conversation and revealed his identity as Messiah. They spoke about issues of ultimate concern. As a result, the woman returned to her village to ask if he might be the Messiah. Her connection to Jesus, established and sustained by conversation, enabled her to have the courage to name her own past and overcome shame that silenced and isolated her, if we think she came to the well at noon due to her lack of social status. (John 4:1-42) In talking together, Jesus altered her worldview, which included a strong view she had of herself that led to her isolation

A conversation with Peter is also instructive. Jesus began by asking all the disciples a question: "Who do the crowds say that I am?" Peter said he was God's Messiah. (Luke 9:18-20) Peter and the other disciples didn't appear to comprehend this flash of insight but a gap opened in their religious worldview to let Jesus demonstrate his identity later, through the transfiguration. (Luke 9:21-35) Peter's worldview was turned upside down.

Dialogue allows two people (or more) to tell each other the truth, as they understand it. Speaking the truth is central to a life of faith. (Ephesians 4:25) These truthful conversations challenge a worldview that's already formed. As another example, the disciples had a certain meaning for the word Messiah. Jesus didn't always conform to their expectations. They had to learn what Messiah meant from the Messiah. In conversation, if we genuinely engage, we tell the truth by giving others our true and best reasons for believing or doing something. These reasons are taken from the warehouse of meaning we call a worldview.

In talking together people convey to each other the personal meanings for ideas, values, feelings and beliefs. As a consequence, it becomes an opportunity to reflect on these meanings and to ask ourselves if these are the assumptions we want to continue to rely upon.

During conversation carried out in Christian community, deep calls to deep: hearts are acquainted with the Heart of God. With trust and truthfulness, conversation allows the meaning we attach to words, values, feelings and beliefs to be transformed in the light of scripture. Questions surface. We put them on the table without fearing rejection or disdain. One heart communes with others: speaking to people and communing with God in spiritual conversation allows us to move closer to Jesus, with help from the Holy Spirit.

Recall that those in spiritual type one, (word oriented) will tend to be less comfortable with truth as a conversation than those who are comfortable in types two or three. Immediate negative reactions to the idea of truth as a conversation must be taken into account when we converse with others. It's easy to feel insulted if someone from style one seems to imply we aren't good Christians unless we use the same words in the same way they do. We must be patient and perceptive. Collaborative theological reflection doesn't rest on suggesting that words of the faith are unimportant, or are slippery concepts we can never be sure about. We need to be clear about the words we use when speaking about Christ and the Church. The issue in collaborative reflection isn't so much about clarity as it is about how people came to the concepts they hold in the first place and also about how people learn.

Conversation educates our worldview. Learning is a dynamic interaction between what people expect and pay attention to; and, since we can't pay attention to everything, it helps us become more aware of what we need to say to others so that they understand us better. Paying attention is an aspect of theological reflection that requires skill, effort and insight.

Paying attention and organizing experience are part of the brain/body work of learning. The outcome of paying attention is stored in memory, from birth onwards.[2] Under ordinary circumstances, new information leaks into a worldview unnoticed until a surprise occurs that can't be ignored because it disrupts elements of that worldview. Jesus surprised Nicodemus, the Samaritan woman, and Peter. When a surprise occurs, however slight or significant, the worldview we've already formed is challenged and may change if we come to value the insights we gain from being surprised. This is normal for the learning process. The learning process we are referring to is depicted in Figure #5.

In order to demonstrate the learning process more fully and apply it to collaborative theological reflection, the following three stories about a man named David (referred to earlier) will illustrate some of the strengths and limitations of personal and collaborative theological reflection, particularly with regard to the relationship between surprise and predictability. In what follows, David's story is presented in three exercises:

- Part A: David's Story [Transmitting a worldview]
- Part B: David's and George's Stories [Informing a worldview]
- Part C: Bongani's Story [Transforming a worldview]

While it remains his story, David engages with two other men. One who lives in his own country, and another who is African. David's encounters with these two men finally draw him into collaborative theological reflection.

As you sift through David's formative experience, you'll notice generative themes. Recall that these themes are moved by universal human needs, personal narratives and global contexts. As you read through each situation, what would you identify as his universal needs, personal narrative and global context? As you identify themes that characterize David's early experience, you'll begin to see what he came to assume and expect as normative for discipleship in the Christian faith. His expectations travel with him into every new experience, as is the case for all of us.

If theological reflection is to become a dialogical conversation, whether it's one we have internally with ourselves or one carried out with others that's collaborative and dialogical, we must take account of expectations. An expectation is a theory we hold about the world and the way it works. People come to every experience with expectations whether or not they're unaware of them or able to state them. If learning is organizing experience, people look for patterns in experience based on their expectations in order to make sense of what's happening and what they think may happen next. As you read about David, record your understanding of the assumptions and expectations that he's bringing to each situation.

## DAVID'S STORY

As a young Christian, David went to camp every summer. At camp, he experienced training that shaped his understanding of discipleship. Each day the camp provided quiet time for private devotions, in addition to time spent in small group Bible Study and campfire worship services. David continued the patterns he learned at camp when he was at home. He was consistent at spending some time each day reading scripture and studying.

At university, he invested his free time in a discipleship approach that included an intense and focused program of scripture reading, memorization, practical evangelism and small group Bible Study. As part of being with the discipleship group, David traveled to other countries on mission trips. After College, he decided to go into full-time ministry. He continued to take discipleship seriously when he became a pastor. In the churches where he served, he used the discipleship model he had developed from his youth. David was effective at helping people in his congregations to invest their leisure time in learning about God by following the intense discipleship process that had been so productive for him.

---

**Questions for self-reflection and discussion**

- What's going on?
- What's important to David?
- How would you describe David?
- What do you know about David?
- What do you need to know about David?

---

When people are learning, they're making meaning and they are using meaning that they made in the past. The meaning we use and make is full of what are called anticipatory constructs. The brain and body are linked during learning through anticipatory constructs that influence how we see the world, based on personal experience. We anticipate what we expect. Anticipatory constructs influence what people pay attention to in a given situation. We pay attention to what we expect and what fits with the meaning we've already made about the God, the world, others and ourselves.

This brain/body relationship includes two systems. There's an afferent system and an efferent system that influences what we expect as well as what we perceive. An afferent system sends signals to the brain from the body (through the senses). The efferent system sends signals to the body from the brain and directs the body in what to pay attention to, including what constitutes information. Learning is a dynamic interaction between what people expect and what they pay attention to as they look for information, since we can't pay attention to everything. Paying attention and organizing experience are part of the brain/body work of learning. The brain is involved in guiding people's expectations about what's going on and what will happen next. The outcome is stored in memory. Memory is like a filing cabinet in the head with small compartments in which bits of information are stored. Learning from experience fills these compartments over time and generates the worldview we're forming, until a surprise occurs.

A worldview (meaning system) is a picture of the world as a whole that every person has as part of being human. It's made up of bits and pieces of the holistic environments in which we were raised. A worldview answers the questions: What's the world really like? What's reality like? Who am I really? Why am I here? Is the world friendly or frightening? Is God friendly or frightening? Some of the identifiable elements of a worldview include the following emotionally laden, cognitively rich, embodied concepts for

- God
- Self
- Faith
- The material world
- Mother — and hence all women
- Father — and hence all men
- Family
- Strangers
- Possessions
- The future
- Ideas e.g. Justice, Fairness, Honesty, Relationship, Truth, Beauty, Hope, Duty

These embodied concepts generate our expectations and are held together in a worldview that's unique to each person but has common elements as well. As an example, specific cultural experiences will contribute certain concepts to the worldview that each member of that cultural group is building. People can reflect on their culture's influence but generally they have to gain some distance from it in order to do so.

Theological reflection compels us to question our

assumptions about our embodied concepts. Concepts in a worldview are embodied concepts because they're acquired in the presence of others who demonstrate the significance they attach to them. We take on embodied concepts while we're with other bodies in a given human culture. They're passed on through culture as memes that convey instructions for appropriate ways to stand, sit, walk, as well as appropriate tones of voice and facial expressions for each situation we find ourselves in. These embodied concepts are heavily laden with experience and emotion and can be triggered easily during theological reflection.

Embodied concepts don't stand alone. They hang together in a worldview. An analogy for a worldview is a spider web. Beliefs and practices may be either bridge lines, from which everything hangs, or foundation lines that give shape and outside limits to the web. Damage to a bridge or foundation lines is destructive to the entire web. Since everyone has a somewhat different web of meaning, conversation places a concept or experience on the table that one person may feel strongly about while another person doesn't feel so strongly. In order to capture this dynamic, it's possible, for example, to ask each person at the table how strongly they feel about a topic or idea on a scale from one to ten, with ten being very important? This is another way that theological reflection can become more collaborative.

As we converse with others, we come to realize that we don't place the same emotional value on the concepts or practices under discussion. Conflict can erupt, or boil on the back burner, when the salience of a concept or idea is not shared, or when we're compelled to re-examine something that's dearly held. During theological reflection, it's important to ask questions of other people (and ourselves) to discover the significance of an idea or concept. To continue with the metaphor, other threads (concepts, ideas or practices) within someone's web of meaning compose the pattern that forms the most visible parts of the web. These threads are more easily repaired than bridge or foundation lines so discussing or challenging them is less serious to one's worldview.

Another analogy for worldview is a story, narrative or myth. The story/narrative/myth analogies are extremely useful as long as the web continues to remind us about the salience of beliefs will differ and warns us that some conversations will be more emotionally challenging than others. If we use the myth analogy, a personal worldview has all the qualities Levi-Strauss attributes to myth in general, as discussed earlier. When we listen to someone's story, we try to perceive how its parts are related to the whole and to listen for recurring themes that show up over a lifetime.

How does change come about during healthy, collaborative theological reflection, as we become aware of the myth or story we tell ourselves about the world? Firstly, new learning influences the worldview that we hold. It adds new information to our mental filing system. If you consider what was said about paying attention, you realize that we tend to pay attention to what fits comfortably into the filing system that's already in place. We resist data that conflict with an already existing worldview. Our thinking is disrupted if a surprise occurs that we can't fit into our worldview but we can't ignore or dismiss it easily either.

When events don't match expectations, people have several options: they may ignore a conflict and pretend it doesn't exist, a move they'll pay a high price for over time. Secondly, they may get frustrated and walk away from the worldview they organized when they were young. In doing so, they often leave behind important relationships. Or thirdly, they may choose to re-organize their existing worldview, an option that requires hard work. Change may take hard work, but the costs of not doing it, by feigning ignorance or walking away, are enormous.

Unhealthy reason is sometimes deployed at the point to diminish the significance of the disruption because the person realizes that hard work must be done and doesn't want to face it or believes they're incapable of facing it. There are costs and benefits to every option—no choice is free of hard work and consequence. Part of growing up into the fullness of God is realized as hard spiritual work is taken on with courage.

When hard spiritual work is faced, a mismatch between expectations and what actually happens shows up as dissonance. In the next story, David experiences dissonance and finds a way to face it with courage.

### MAKING SENSE OF DISSONANCE

If we want to understand how dissonance affects David, it helps to see how dissonance shows up in scripture. When Jesus went to Nazareth, Luke 4:14-30, something bad happened. First we read: "He taught in their synagogues, and everyone praised him." (verse 15) Then, "all the people in the synagogue were furious when they heard this. They got up, drove him out of the town, and took him to the brow of the hill on which the town was built, in order to throw him down the cliff. But he walked right through the crowd and went on his way." (verses 28-30) What happened between verse 15 and 28?

Dissonance is an essential dynamic of the teaching/learning relation. Being a teacher is more than writing learning objectives, carrying out a lesson plan or leading learners through a method. To teach is to understand the dynamics of dissonance. Jesus is a teacher and was masterful at these dynamics. If we ask what happened in Nazareth, the answer is dissonance. People expected Jesus to be on their side. When he spoke about foreigners positively they couldn't understand or organize what he said into their existing worldviews. They had a theory about life that he didn't affirm. They had a serious emotional reaction to his words and to him. Dissonance led to violence: they sensed that Jesus' account of the past undermined what they thought should be obvious to him, i.e., that they alone mattered to God.

Dissonance is a disconnection or lack of fit between what people expect and what happens. In dissonance, an anticipatory theory or expectation fails in its predictive role and a whole system seems out of whack.[3] Normally, theory guides understanding in the following way: as we learn, our experience is shaped by essential conditions of life; learning goes on in an environment—in it, because of it and in interaction with it.

People learn by connecting and adapting to their environment. If an event doesn't' fit with their worldview (personal or communal), learners might choose to become interested in its lack of fit and may allow themselves to be carried forward by all the following: curiosity, desire for a solution, pleasure in the search and the journeying itself. In this case, learners enjoy feeling they're learning something. That is, learning expands on what's already known. But on the other hand, they might reject the new information and react to it, as did the people in Nazareth.

Yet even under favorable conditions, when people welcome new information, whenever there's disruption, they face a loss of some kind. If they continue to learn from a situation and recover their balance, they do so by acknowledging the significance of loss. Recovery is never a simple return to a prior state; understanding is enriched by the disruption, but the new situation is never exactly what they experienced when they were young. The lost son is a good example. He came back to the farm and saw it in a new light. He saw his father in a new way, as did the older brother. People learn by sensing their emotional reaction to an event (leaving home), listening to and observing it (being away), getting interested in and curious about it (coming to their senses), and figuring out what they really want to do and who they really want to be (returning home).

When the disruption is overcome, people acquire more awareness of their environment. New information or a new perspective is achieved. Becoming conscious of a loss of fit and recovering our understanding of what's going on are materials out of which we form new purposes or clarify and commit more strongly to purposes we already hold. If there's a disruption, emotion is a conscious sign of a break between the learner's experience and anticipatory theory (whether actual or feared) and what's really happening. Discord sparks reflection. The desire to recover from a destabilizing event converts emotion into curiosity. If people get curious about what might happen next, they become interested in what's going on. That interest refocuses their attention so that they look in new directions and at new data. As a result, they regard a destabilizing event in a fresh way. Their reflection is incorporated into their understanding so that it's enlarged; they can begin to recover. And curiosity plays a key role in that recovery.

If people care about recovery, they don't shun moments of resistance and tension or try to push destabilizing events off a cliff. The point is significant for theological reflection. We cultivate disruptions, not for their own sake but because of their potential to bring to consciousness an experience that's more unified, total and can take more of reality into account. At no point does learning require people to abandon faith in order to recover. Rather, they need to understand Christianity more fully and follow Jesus more closely. As they reflect theologically on disruption, people who are fully alive will adopt the past and make friends even with their blind spots and stupidity, using them as a warning for the future so that they increase their awareness of life. For those who are fully alive, the future isn't ominous; it's a promise and consists of possibilities.

In the following scenario, David encounters dissonance in a ministry setting. He chooses to become collaborative rather than sticking to his old perceptions. He has an opportunity to reflect on the worldview he constructed out of personal experience when he was first learning what it means to follow Jesus.

### DAVID'S AND GEORGE'S STORIES

At one church, David was surprised by a man, George, who was involved in church but showed no interest in being a disciple following the pattern David had used elsewhere.

David was sure that George was a sincere Christian; he led worship but never came to the structured discipleship opportunities David organized for people in the Church. David and George were friends. George was committed to exercising his gifts in the church and would drop in at unexpected times and sit in David's office or they would go for coffee. David was puzzled. He felt uncomfortable with George's lack of spiritual discipline. George didn't fit the model David had for his own life-expectations he had always relied on.

In thinking about the situation, David met with colleagues to ask if they knew people like George. They did and outlined some of the common elements between their situations and the one David faced.

After the conversation, David began to reflect on his relationship with George by asking himself questions about his assumptions concerning discipleship. After considering his own pattern, he decided to try involving George in a more relaxed approach to discipleship. If George asked a question or expressed interest in a topic, David would follow up with responses that led them both further into scripture. At times, they prayed together.

Over the next few years, David and George covered a lot of topics and David felt that they were making progress. George continued to raise topics and ask questions. Their spiritual friendship continued until David moved on from that church to a church development assignment in southern Africa.

---

**Questions for self-reflection and discussion**

- What's going on?
- What's important to David and to George?
- How would you describe David and George?
- What do you know about David and George?
- What do you need to know about David and George?

---

George surprised David. He understood aspects of George's behavior, labeling them Christian, but couldn't incorporate other aspects into his expectations for a Christian lifestyle.

In order for David to understand George, he had to move laterally and expand his horizon to include George as someone who was living a faithful Christian life. He had to learn to trust him even though George didn't act in the same ways David did. He had to ask questions that enabled him to see George anew and interpret George without partiality for the particular way of life he had learned to associate with Christianity. David had to loosen his grip on that way of life without letting go of what it means to be a person of faith. The accommodations David had to make were personal. In conversation with them, his colleagues helped him expand his understanding of the Christian life.

As we grow up we all face the situation that David was in: aspects of new experience cause us to challenge our worldviews to some degree. As an example, if confronted by dissonance in a university setting, a young adult may reconsider the validity of their own worldview, or perhaps, components of it. Whether they change or ignore the challenge seems to depend on:

- The strength of their already existing worldviews
- The degree of pressure from credible, reliable external sources
- Their own sense of discomfort with the challenge
- The perceived benefits and costs of changing their view
- The possibility of change remains, though seems to lessen as a person ages
- Yet most people deny they are influenced by external elements and possess a charmingly simplistic notion that they are sensitive to efforts to influence them and are vigilant in screening out these influences.[4]

As people age, it becomes less easy to alter an existing worldview. With age, people may have more experiences to organize into a worldview that helps them to predict what might happen in familiar situations.

Yet dissonance can be so disturbing that they may choose to walk away from the worldview they got when they were young, rather than reflecting on it and asking themselves what's really going on. If people walk away from a worldview they constructed when they were young, (which sometimes includes abandoning loved ones) they tell themselves a new story about the world—a story that has to cover up or calm down the effects of dissonance.

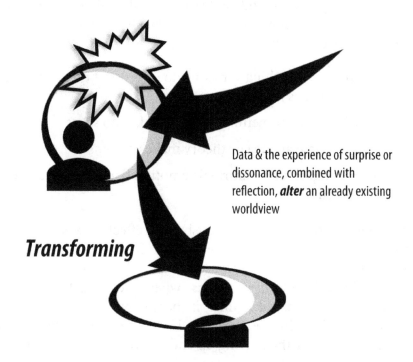

Data & the experience of surprise or dissonance, combined with reflection, *alter* an already existing worldview

*Transforming*

Theological reflection must acknowledge the dynamics of learning if it's to become an effective way to address destabilizing situations and the problems it raises. A problem is an event that doesn't easily fit into the worldview we've developed over time. The event may offer us something new we've never experienced before so that there's an insufficient anticipatory framework for understanding what's going on. Or, it may trigger a traumatic past event. A trauma is an experience that's too complex for the personality to handle.

In either case, a problem presents us with a surprise that doesn't make sense due to the way we've learned to think about the world. We experience dissonance based on the way we've tended to process and perceive data. When we're surprised, and can't resolve the differences involved, we experience dissonance between our worldview and what's happening. We experience dissonance due to ways we perceive and process information.

Depending on individual learning styles, dissonance may occur from the following ways of processing and perceiving information, e.g., through

- Doing: something someone does or won't do (including you) makes no sense
- Observing: something you see makes no sense
- Thinking: an idea or theory makes no sense
- Feeling: an uncomfortable emotion flares up and makes no sense

If we face dissonance courageously, we reflect on what's going on. Emotion is resolved as we recover from loss and acquire deeper meaning for what previously we couldn't fathom.

Theological reflection begins when we're disturbed. All critical thinking is like this: it begins with an emotional disturbance in what we expect. If we want to learn from experience, rather than giving up and walking away, we learn to reflect theologically so as to gradually or suddenly incorporate spiritual and biblical insights into a worldview so that it can sustain us through the crises of life.

Worldviews are personal, idiosyncratic constructions that need repair and new parts in order to provide shelter for us in the storms of life. One of the main benefits of facing a destabilizing event, and working through it, comes about when we see blind spots we were oblivious to previously and begin to test the feasibility of what we always thought was impossible. The illustration on the previous page captures the transforming effects of surprise.

### THEOLOGY IS A MATTER OF UNDERSTANDING

Surprise and predictability are important in learning. A surprise occurs if what we expect doesn't happen or when what we expect fails to happen. Reconsider the scenario of Jesus' visit to Nazareth in Luke 4.14-30. How does this event in Nazareth help to understand David's reaction to George? In general, the accumulation of good theories about what's going on helps us mature as followers of Jesus. A theory is an accumulation of experience from many people, seen from a long way off and organized into a generalized form. It's built from a broad perspective, based on wide experience and reveals common patterns and general agreement, though it's not necessarily universal. A good theory is good because it explains experience aptly. In this way, dissonance threatens theory because it seems to suggest that our theory is incorrect.

Unlike the situation in Nazareth, under favorable conditions, dissonance teaches us something new but always poses a question of how the new information will fit with information that's already there. As we continue to read the New Testament, we learn that some people turned their dissonant emotion into interest and followed Jesus all the way to the cross and beyond, as witnesses of his resurrection. In this move, they altered their own environment. New possibilities, new realities emerged for them and for the whole world.

If people learn to understand their environment, folding new insight into their view of it, they gain stability that's essential to living well. In general, we form purposes and learn about life by becoming conscious of losses of fit between what we expect and what actually happens. As we recover from loss, we gain new understanding. Theological reflection enables the acquisition of this new understanding during a dialogical conversation aimed at becoming conscious of our losses and recovering from them, in communities of truth.

Those who eventually came to understand Jesus allowed their theories about Messiah to be challenged. They began to see the whole world in terms of God's love. Their theories, like old wineskins, were replaced by new ones that Christ's death and resurrection filled with new wine. They allowed disruption to bring new life. Theological reflection is a high calling, extended to every believer. Through the process, we're welcomed into dialogue during a conversation God initiates with us; which is sustained and strengthened through the Holy Spirit and supported by what we see in Christ's example.

Theological reflection should be a conversation that compels us to engage with other worldviews that differ from our own and calls us to love others, even as God loves us. As Jesus said, "If you love those who love you, what reward will you get?...If you greet only your own people [who think like you] what are you doing more than others? ...Be perfect, therefore, even as your heavenly father is perfect." (Matt. 5:47-48).

If people "greet their own people only" they tend to stay with what makes sense to them and reject what makes no sense. Jesus made no sense to the people in Nazareth; at least, he made no sense if he was a good old local boy who knew how to please people by saying what they wanted to hear. Jesus' words forced them to consider their way of looking at the world. At first, they only reacted in anger. That reaction is to be expected as we introduce ideas or behaviour that doesn't match the ideas and behavior of people we converse with theologically. Yet there were some who finally got what he was saying and accepted him as Messiah. They came to hear and see who Jesus is and what he wanted them to understand. Jesus can still transform worldviews through conversation. People with ears to hear and eyes to see find a Savior in Jesus Christ.

What about David? How did his initial experience, and the worldview formed by that experience, shape his developing capacity to work with others who also wanted to know Jesus? It's only through linking our hearts with the Heart of God that we're renewed in the way we perceive the world. The process of that renewal is available to us and it's our work to collaborate with others until we come to see and hear the whole counsel of God.

One way forward is by learning to reflect on the worldview we currently hold and that holds us. Reflection depends on doing the spiritual work of feeling, talking and listening to God, other people and ourselves.

## THE IMPORTANCE OF FEELING, TALKING, LISTENING

If we think carefully about collaboration, we must ask some questions. Did David actually listen to George? Did he allow himself to learn from George? Was David putting in time until George got to be like him? Did David adequately challenge George to begin an integrated, disciplined way of life? The potential for listening and for collaborating with other people is developed (or not) when we're young. A great deal depends on the environment we experienced as children and the expectations people had for us, as well as those we have for ourselves. To understand the skills involved in conversing (or their lack) let's consider what all children learn or fail to learn when they are young.

David Wood (1998) discussed the potential children have to learn to think as they converse with teachers or other adults. He made his observations by comparing Piaget and Vygotsky, two theorists mentioned earlier. Piaget and Vygotsky disagreed with each other about the potential children have to converse with adults and each other, which was a disagreement over different assumptions they held about the relationship between talking and thinking and about what it means to know something.

For Piaget, intellectual competence referred to what someone could do unassisted; for Vygotsky a fundamental feature of intelligence included the capacity to learn through instruction and with assistance, what he referred to as the capacity developed through a zone of proximal development.[5] In this zone, the child's potential to learn is revealed and realized in interactions with more knowledgeable people. For Vygotsky, cooperatively achieved success lay at the heart of all learning and development.[6] The zone of proximal learning is ground on which learners and teachers grow together.[7] Collaborative knowledge passes between them, as it's "embodied in the actions, work, play, technology, literature, art and talk of members of a society."[8]

In contrast, Piaget emphasizes the abstract quality of language. He thought that language exerted no formative effects on the structure of thinking but rather was a medium or method of representation in which thought took place. For him, mental work (thinking) is derived from action, not talk.[9] Piaget did link talking and thinking to say that "although language does not create the structure of thinking, it does facilitate its emergence," and suggested that through talking to others, particularly other children, a child's thinking became socialized; but "although children talk as they play together, they don't, according to Piaget, really converse."[10] Piaget's bias toward individualism (learning is what one does by oneself) may have led him to dismiss links between talking, thinking, acting and learning to converse.

For Vygotsky, childhood speech wasn't personal but was social and communicative both in origin and intent.[11] He analyzed research that led Piaget to make his claim that children don't converse and came away with a different interpretation. To him, speech served two different functions: in the beginning speech served a regulative, communicative function. Later it served other functions and transformed the way children learn, think and understand. To him, talking is an instrument or tool of thought, not only providing a code or system for representing the world but also the means by which self-regulation comes about, i.e., the sort of skill experienced monks excel at, if you reflect on their disciplined soulful thinking.

On Vygotsky's view of language, the initial motivation for gesture and speech is to regulate the world through the agency of other people and our need for them. Gestures and speech serve this role. To him, speech, like any system of movement, is a physical activity, a way of controlling one's body to achieve goals and avoid discomfort. For him, "the overt activity of speaking provides the basis for 'inner speech', that rather mysterious covert activity that often forms the process of thinking."[12] Inner speech or thinking has its basis in talking, which implies that physical actions plus the physical activity of speaking are eventually internalized so that they create verbal thinking.

Vygotsky considered all forms of thought to be actions. To him, the children's talk that Piaget recorded is "midway between the social and intellectual functions of speech, [since] the child who is talking to himself is regulating and planning his own activities in ways that foreshadow verbal thinking."[13] The process is recursive.

As a particular male toddler discovers how to regulate the actions of others through speech, his developing knowledge of language acts back on him so that others can regulate his actions through their speech. As he discovers how to gain peoples' attention by speaking, and learns how to direct their attention to features of the shared physical world—to solicit specific action and services, inhibit, refuse and so forth—he's subject to the same sort of regulation in the speech of others. Others begin to regulate and direct his attention, solicit his services and inhibit his activities.[14] Social power operates in the give and take of conversing.

Speech forms the higher mental processes, including the ability to plan, evaluate, memorize and reason. These processes are formed through social interaction. Looked at this way, talking doesn't simply reflect or represent concepts already formed at a non-verbal level. It structures and directs the process of thinking itself. To Vygotsky, talk is a product of social experience and evidence for the emergence of intellectual self-control.[15]

How does this theory influence theological reflection? It has a lot of impact. We learn as children whether or not we have a voice worth hearing, whether or not what we say matters to anyone else. Some children learn that their voice matters more than anyone else's, or learn they have to fight to be heard. As a result, they argue but don't converse. Some people learn it's dangerous to say what they think and this fear may be common. Every time a conversation begins, or even before it starts, social power is exercised by everyone present and exerts itself perhaps by asserting the right to state every thought that comes to mind or by withholding thought in order to feel safe.

Everyone in a group has already learned whether or not it's possible for them to speak the truth in love when they're with other people. Theological reflection opens up a possibility for learning and unlearning many things we came to believe as children—about God, others and ourselves.

In the first story, David accepted a model for discipleship based on what he did on his own, as an individual. In the second story, he shifted slightly due to his experience with George but didn't challenge his own fundamental assumptions. While they talked to each other, it wasn't a collaborative experience since they never actively engaged in talking about how to talk together.

Collaboration invites participants to change the worldview each one brings to the conversation. If David and George collaborated, both would change in some way. New insights and commitments would emerge. Perhaps David merely accommodated George and didn't see how to collaborate with him. It's a common mistake in leadership that arises when power relationships are under-analyzed by well-meaning leaders and followers and when believers don't hold each other accountable or make their own needs as clear as they are able to do.

### Dialogue enhances personal formation

Power is exercised in every social relation. In terms of the power games involved in their relationship, George won from one perspective. He changed very little. He kept David at bay. But he lost overall. We can only surmise how practices commonly associated with Christianity might have impacted him in ways he would have been eternally grateful to know. David and George played a game of imposing and resisting but didn't use power to bring something new into being. David and George regulated each other through their use of power, but to what end? Again, they'd learned to use social power when they were very young and didn't consider discussing social power itself to be part of healthy theological conversation.

### Social power is exercised every time we talk

Through the use of non-verbal communication, infants negotiate social encounters by regulating the level and amount of social stimulation to which they're subjected. Babies can avert their gaze, shut their eyes, stare past someone, become glassy-eyed and refuse to engage. Through a decisive use of gaze behaviors, babies can reject, distance themselves from, or defend themselves against their parents or strangers. They can also reinitiate engagement whenever they desire, through gazing, smiling or vocalizing. Autonomy and independence operate in all social interactions that regulate the quality or quantity of engagement.[16] George and David were regulating the quality of their interaction through the use of social power and non-verbal communication. Were they conscious of the effects they had on each other?

Every conversation is dangerous. In a healthy conversation, as they're talking together, people have freedom to deny meaning and take responsibility for what they say. When it's healthy, people engage in a bearable degree of self-revelation. But to be held accountable for every sign our lips and bodies convey would paralyze us. The possibility of being pinned to an utterance emerges as soon as we begin to talk together. Suppose you're in a conversation with another person. You make a comment. The other person replies. "But you said..." You reply by saying, "I didn't say that... I said..." What's eventually accepted as the truth between you is influenced by the play of social power between you.

The social power exercised as people converse is significant. If we write an assignment or a letter to someone, our thoughts are private and shaped to fit a particular audience, e.g., a teacher of friend. If we talk together, our thoughts enter the public domain.

This is precisely how talking together establishes shared narratives and forms worldviews that are understood by members of a group. It's powerful and liberating when a group suddenly realizes they share the same grief or worry. But how does that shared narrative act back on those who speak? The power of talking together builds solidarity. But its emergence also threatens personal authenticity and our differences from one another. From a leader's perspective, this is a crucial issue in theological reflection. The power of speaking is different from the power of writing. We need to attend to group dynamics with great sensitivity. Listening well is a first step.

When dialogical conversation is working well,

listening[17] enables participants to narrate their worldview (or bits of it) in order to organize knowledge and become conscious of it, while maintaining authenticity (being distant and different) and solidarity (being near and similar to the rest of the group).

Healthy theological reflection makes it possible for people to be intimately connected (socially near) but to remain different from one another, as was necessary for those engaged in the example we used about consuming alcohol in the application of Theological Model #3. Being near and different is one way to express what it means to obey Jesus Christ, to think critically and to love others in Christ's name. What's it like to be near people and yet remain different from them? Jesus came to us. He was near to us and different from us—the lesson of the Incarnation. What's the evidence that David and George worked out what it means to be socially close and yet authentically distinct from one another?

Healthy theological conversation is modeled on the Incarnation. We aren't divine, as Jesus is, but we can learn to be near and open to legitimate differences in each other. Talking together is empowering in an environment that's open and flexible. Speaking is educational if understanding is achieved. Understanding is creative when it's based on accurate awareness. When "we are accurately aware of someone else's sensations, thoughts, feelings, wants and the meaning of their actions, [we] are truly aware of that person."[18] Part of listening has to do with our willingness and ability both to lead and follow the person we're trying to understand. Artful Listening has instructions to guide those who listen to someone tell a story about a destabilizing event. But other aspects in listening also matter during collaborative theological dialogue.

Listening is always the activity of following another person's story and developing a full understanding of the narrative in a way they would acknowledge as accurate. Getting with the meaning of another person's narrative is hard work and implies paying attention to body language, non-verbal signs, as well as intentions and words. Solidarity or getting with others may be understood as building rapport.

In rapport we ask how much basic similarity, harmony or alignment there is between two people. Rapport is built through affect attunement or pre-verbal communication that infants know how to convey. This is a shared activity in which listeners and speakers become expert at aligning their pre-verbal meanings with one another. Along with rapport, trust is crucial to achieving understanding between two people. Trust is confidence that accumulates during an encounter and isn't determined through language alone. It's based on reading body language. The "sharing of affective states is the most persuasive...feature of inter-subjective relatedness" in which "empathetic responsiveness" is achieved and trust develops.[19]

Empathetic responsiveness and affect attunement entail sending and receiving messages between a listener and another person. As an example, the

- Listener reads the other's affective state from their behavior

- Listener mirrors but doesn't imitate the behavior so as to convey that the affective state is understood to belong to an inner experience of the other

- Those listened to read accurately that their inner affective state is sensed and their behavior is not merely copied[20]

While empathy involves realizing what someone is trying to say, affect attunement is empathy's bodily counterpart. To be in the presence of empathy helps people understand their own felt sense and how it is constructed. The willingness to lead and follow as people talk together is further expressed through the issue of self-regulation.

Rapport, trust and self-regulation are three dimensions of talking together that encourage dialogue. Control is shared if both parties lead and follow. In following, listeners allow others to tell their stories in their own way. In leading, listeners may get others to tell their stories in the way that a listening leader wants them to be presented. The listener's intentions are paramount in the issue of social control. Three possibilities for control during an encounter exist; which are

- Leading by persuading
- Clarifying by directing
- Discovering by attending

In persuasion, the listener leads. The outcome of talk is a reduction of the quality of data and an increase in the speaker's resistance. As a result, rapport and trust are undermined and control is high. In directing, the listener wants to clarify the story. We clarify when we want talk to be more efficient and do so by asking questions. While questions are useful, and differ in their degree of control, they shape the direction of conversation. Even with the best of intentions, these questions may lead the one speaking away from key information.

While there are times when the searching aspect of clarifying talk is important, the one asking questions has the most control over the direction of the talk. If the listener's intention is to discover the story the one talking wants to tell, the listener lets the one talking speak spontaneously. Letting people tell their own story may even save time. Most people can tell their stories in two to four minutes. If left to do so, the one talking provides a complete cycle for the story. The listener is able to pick up emotional hot spots and issues that are authentic to the one whose story it is. The aim of listening is to get with someone so as to get their whole story, attending to them is the quickest way to accomplish that aim. The secret of listening is to give full attention to another person. As one moves from persuasion to attending, rapport and trust increase and control is shared.[21] In an atmosphere of complete attention, trust flourishes.

As people are talking together, their conversation may be based on personal or collaborative reflection. Personal reflection is a developed capacity to catch ourselves acting and believing in certain ways. As we catch ourselves, we ask whether we want to continue to behave in this way. It's something we do by ourselves. Collaborative reflection is cooperative inquiry into what we're thinking and doing that helps consider how we want to act and think in the future. The problem under investigation, a destabilizing event, is personal; it's someone's real problem.

### COLLABORATIVE THEOLOGICAL INQUIRY

Collaborative reflection involves other people in constructing an interpretation of reality using everyone's accumulated experience so that we don't get a perspective on situations from one person's view only. Yet each person involved can maintain integrity, if they're clear about their point of view and if they're willing and able to learn from other people.

Collaborative reflection is a conjoint educational activity so that everyone

- Speaks and listens
- Invests in addressing the situation
- Articulates their perspective on the situation's meaning
- Collaborates on envisioning/imagining possible ways forward

Personal and collaborative reflection each provide balance for the other. While personal theological reflection carries particular limitations that might de-rail genuine inquiry if they go unchecked, the dynamics of social power are a factor in collaborative theological reflection that must be addressed. Collaborative and personal processes of reflection balance each other's excesses if they inform one another by

- Revealing blind spots inherent in someone's personal reflection
- Allowing personal authenticity to limit the misuse of social power in groups

- Searching personally and collaboratively for the mind of Christ on any issue.

When they're used interdependently, personal and collaborative reflection each creates and balances wise and liberating theological reflection. Expectations are challenged and affirmed. The process for discovering how or to what extent everyone agrees or differs on the problem requires an activity in which we make it abundantly clear how each of us is currently seeing the web of meaning that's presented along with a destabilizing situation.

In collaborative theological inquiry, extra effort must be directed toward unpacking the situation that the group is trying to understand. The whole group needs to be clear about what's going on. In addition, people need to express that understanding openly to one another so that the conversation is on a solid footing.

The next chapter includes descriptions of educational practices that allow a group to be certain they understand the given situation fully and in the same way. While people bring different points of view to what's going on, it's essential that the group clarify to each other their perceptions of the inner workings, the sequencing of events and the overall picture that the situation implies. Doing this work collaboratively depends on careful linguistic and non-linguistic representations of the situation. The representational approaches in the next chapter are a format for building clarity among a group of people as they reflect theologically on a destabilizing event.

# Notes

1. Parker Palmer, *The Courage to Teach* (San Francisco: Jossey-Bass, 1998), 95.

2. John Dewey, *Art as Experience* (New York: A Perigee Book, 1980).

3. *Art as Experience*, 19.

4. George Barna, *Transforming Children into Spiritual Champions*, Ventura, CA: Regal, 2003, 59.

5. David Wood, *How Children Think and Learn* Second Edition (Oxford: Blackwell, 1998), 26.

6. *How Children Think*, 27.

7. J.E. Bellous, "Spirituality and Ethical Orality in Children: Educating an oral self," for the *International Journal of Children's Spirituality*, Cathy Ota (Ed.) Chichester Institute of Higher Education, (Chichester, England: Vol. 5, No. 1, June: 9-26), 7-9.

8. *How Children Think*, 7.

9. *How Children Think*, 28.

10. *How Children Think*, 28.

11. *How Children Think*, 29.

12. *How Children Think*, 29.

13. *How Children Think*, 29-30.

14. *How Children Think*, 30.

15. *How Children Think*, 31.

16. Daniel Stern, *The Interpersonal World of the Infant* (New York: Basic Books, 2000), 22.

17. S Miller, et al, *Connecting with Self and Other* (Littleton, Colorado: Interpersonal Communications Programs, 1988).

18. *Connecting*, 173.

19. *The Interpersonal World*, 138.

20. *The Interpersonal World*, 139.

21. *Connecting*, 173-202.

## CHAPTER 8

# THEOLOGICAL REFLECTION AND
# REPRESENTING MEANING

I f we review the process that's used with the models of theological reflection in Chapter One, and ask how this process applies to collaborative theological reflection, the first step of the process (establish the situation) shows up as a bigger problem than it does in personal theological reflection. Here's the question: How will a group of people with very different personal experiences, religious views, or cultural perspectives get together on what's going on in a given situation? In particular, in collaborative theological reflection, the aim is to find an agreed-upon explanation of what's going on so that scripture, tradition and insight can be employed when deciding what to do in response to it. To begin, all those involved in the collaboration need to discover and express their own understanding of the situation. How might that be accomplished?

When people try to capture an element of their personal worldview and its influence on the way they interpret a destabilizing event, they may choose to convey their knowledge in one of two ways—linguistically or non-linguistically. To convey their perspectives, and acquire new information, the group as a whole must agree on what participants see in the situation at hand. In collaboration, the whole group gathers data as a way to get clear about what's going on. Acquiring new information happens most effectively if a group understands and sees what each one already knows about a situation.

The two primary ways to represent knowledge we already have and that we want to use in theological reflection, is to work linguistically, by using words, or non-linguistically, by using visual images. This chapter focuses on non-linguistic patterns for getting clear data about a situation, in addition to more typical linguistic approaches people commonly use. When a group is working towards theological reflection on a destabilizing event, it's essential to express the situation linguistically and non-linguistically so that all those invested in addressing the situation are on the same page as to what the problem is, how it came about and what's included in it.

## LINGUISTIC REPRESENTATION

Linguistic representations of current knowledge take the forms of words, sentences or stories about what we already know. As an example of a linguistic representation of what's going on, suppose we asked a 5 year-old child to tell us what happens when people eat food. In response to our question, he tells a story about how there are little men inside our bodies and each little man has a small bucket. When we eat a mouthful of food, each bucket gets a bite. Then some pulleys and ropes let the buckets down into our stomachs.

It's a child's interpretation about what happens as we eat and it's an elaborate linguistic representation of what the child imagines. Some research suggests that linguistic knowledge may be stored as statements in long-term memory. We access this knowledge by speaking, telling a story or explaining what we think about a subject. In theological reflection, it's important to let people tell their stories about God, the church, other people and themselves. If you recall the second model for *Lectio Divina*, this is what's involved in working through the five sections of the practice. We tell our stories and listen to God's story and compare the differences.

## NON-LINGUISTIC REPRESENTATION

Non-linguistic representations are line drawings that capture what we think. We can do more than tell stories to convey knowledge because what we know and have already experienced isn't just organized in words, sentences or stories. We store data in images that form particular patterns. These patterns can be retrieved if we consider relationships between one idea and another. Educational theorist Robert Marzano (et al)[1] identified strategies for representing non-linguistic knowledge that we have stored in memory. His patterns are the basis for the versions presented in this chapter that have been derived from his work.

Non-linguistic models allow people to organize their mental pictures, or ideas, according to a topic, time, cause and effect, episode, principle, or concept. It's quite remarkable to note big differences among participants as they begin to draw their perceptions of what's going on in a situation.

The first nine diagrams show visually how to structure a whole group's understanding of a situation. Following the nine diagrams, there is a summary of Marzano's explanations of the pictographic representations, mental images, and physical models depicted in the chapter. At the end of the chapter, there are specific examples of these non-linguistic ways to represent meaning based on biblical examples.

### DIAGRAM #1 ORGANIZING A DESCRIPTIVE PATTERN

This pattern represents facts about a person, place, thing or event, not necessarily in any given order.

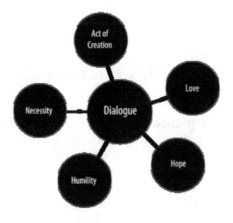

## Diagram #2 Organizing by a Sequence of Time

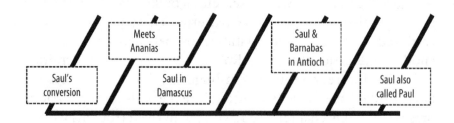

**DIAGRAM #3 ORGANIZING BY CAUSE AND EFFECT**

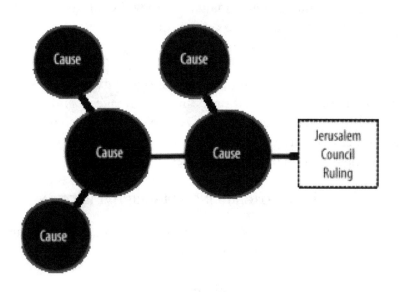

**DIAGRAM #4 ORGANIZING BY DESCRIBING AN EPISODE**

Collect data around events that include a setting, time, place, people, duration, sequence and particular cause and effect.

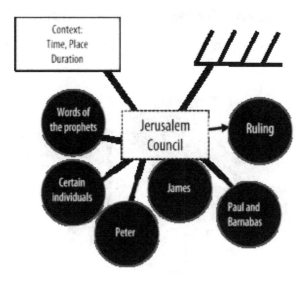

**DIAGRAM #5 ORGANIZING BASED ON GENERALIZATIONS OR PRINCIPLES**

This pattern includes a general statement and supporting examples.

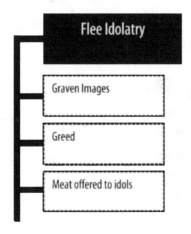

**DIAGRAM # 6 ORGANIZING BY CONCEPT**

These patterns organize data around a concept and given examples.

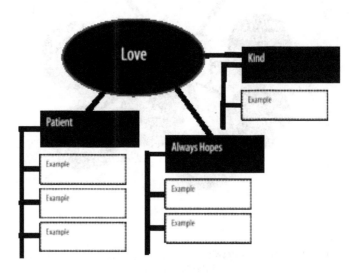

**DIAGRAM # 7 ORGANIZING BY CONCEPT**

This pattern gives an analysis of a word that shows its category and a distinguishing feature.

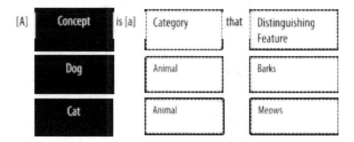

**DIAGRAM #8 ORGANIZING BY CONCEPT**

This pattern organizes a word or phrase by separating out its conceptual dimensions, showing the relationships among those dimensions and arriving at a working hypothesis for the concept.

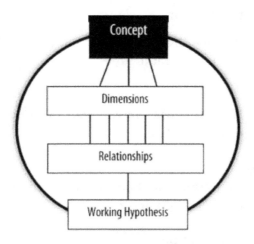

**DIAGRAM #9 ORGANIZING WITH A CONCEPT MAP**

This pattern captures one's current thinking about a topic. The lines between the centre and the circles form a relationship. State the proposition that connect the concept to the words that explain it more fully from your perspective.

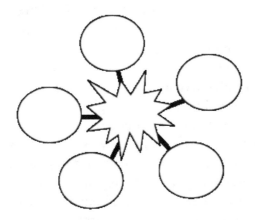

## Pictographic Representations

To offer a pictographic representation of an idea you have in mind, you might draw one of the following images:

- A human skeleton
- The story that the five year old told about what happens to food when we eat it
- The solar system
- My Community (Ask people to draw a diagram of the place where they live)

## Mental Images

This representation of knowledge attempts to capture abstract content. You might draw

- A physics equation
- A line drawing of basic shapes that convey the essence of a mental picture

## Physical Models

These representations are physical objects that people use to show what they know. If someone knows how to count, wooden blocks can be used to show that knowledge. Three-dimensional figures can be used to convey spiritual experiences, as Jerome Berryman does in his book *Godly Play.*

Using physical models reveals what someone knows but learning is most effective if new data is added while that physical demonstration is going on. In using physical models, people may discover new data as they manipulate these objects or someone else may show them something new as they engage with them. In either case, new and old knowledge is integrated. As examples, people might create Paper Mache representations or build a wall out of blocks to convey an idea about a passage of scripture. If people use non-linguistic representation (visual images) they should also express their meaning in words after the physical model is created.

## Kinesthetic Representations

We can also convey what we know using our bodies through physical movement of some kind. For example, we can role-play or express emotion facially. We might dance out a conflict we're having or that we think someone else is having with us. As an example, liturgical dance is used to communicate feelings, thoughts and impressions during worship and conveys what can't be said in words.

In general, anyone engaged in non-linguistic representation should also be given an opportunity and the responsibility to express their meaning in words and conversation, to the extent that they can. In collaborative theological reflection, a group of people work together on representing a destabilizing event both linguistically and non-linguistically until everyone believes the essentials of the problem have been laid out and a variety of perspectives are presented.

---

**EXERCISE: REPRESENTATION OF MEANING**

To get the most out of this material, go back to Jake or Marjorie's stories in section one and, using one of the above non-linguistic representational methods, construct images that illustrate one or more dimensions of the stories that Jake and Marjorie are telling themselves and others.

Can you use another form of non-linguistic representation to illustrate what you have learned so far about David's stories?

---

# Notes

1.  The representational models used in this chapter are adapted from R. J. Marzano et al., *Classroom Instruction that Works*.

## CHAPTER 9

# AN APPROACH TO COLLABORATIVE
# THEOLOGICAL REFLECTION

hy should we engage in collaborative theological
reflection? Imagine the following scenario. In a rural
community, First Church is located next door to a
seniors' housing complex. At a church Board meeting, the pastor
introduced an agenda item that received significant resistance
from members of the Board. The item concerned the seniors'
complex. She wanted the Board to agree to start a ministry with
the seniors who were in residence. Board members refused to
consider the possibility of carrying out that ministry. One
member commented to another after the meeting that he was
frustrated because it was the first time he'd heard about the idea.
He complained that, if the pastor wanted buy-in, she needed to
tell Board members in advance about the idea before she comes
with it all laid out and planned. What went wrong? Is ministry to
seniors a good idea?

The resistance and refusal this pastor experienced could have
been prevented if she'd begun a different way with the members
of her Board. Perhaps her idea received rejection because she
didn't work out what the whole group would bring to this
possibility. She introduced a new idea to the group without
engaging in collaborative theological reflection.

Leaders often introduce ideas that don't receive adequate
buy-in. They think about their work twenty-four hours a day,
seven days a week, or so it feels to them. They also may feel
it's their job to do the work themselves. It's what they get paid

to do. While it may seem to other people that they're bossy or controlling, internally, they may feel burdened by a sense of responsibility they don't know how to convey to other people. From a pastor's point of view, no one else invests the same amount of time envisioning the future or has the same access to information that pastors have available. As a result, leaders frequently run ahead of their followers. In order to bring everyone along, this pastor needed to work collaboratively in the visioning process. Not to do so is to meet a stream of resistance from people who also care deeply about the church and their community. [Of course, resistance can have different and less noble reasons and motivations behind it.]

Under favorable conditions, in collaboration, people work on a situation together. Notice in the scenario described above that the pastor didn't bring a situation to the Board. She brought a solution. What would have happened if she'd done some homework and presented the situation that the seniors next door found themselves in? For example, what if there were a number of seniors next door who belonged to the same denomination of First Church? How might data the pastor brought to the group allowed Board members to get clear about a situation that existed right next door? How might beginning this way have drawn them forward to respond compassionately so that they saw for themselves that it was a situation in which they could take some action? In addition, it would have been action they had genuine interest in; one ideally that they could prayerfully consider in light of the other commitments that the Board had already taken on.

In collaboration, people have time to consider a situation, and its needs, and also have the opportunity to reflect on current commitments and the general program of the church. They also have a chance to be creative and responsive to a situation they begin to own. In the process, they come with ideas and insights and talk together until they realize what everyone is bringing to the situation. They work on issues together until they have a way to be inclusive of all the important aspects of the situation that, with research, they've been able to identify. They may refuse to work at envisioning a way forward until they hear from everyone and thoroughly understand the situation and what it might call for; but when they each personally own the situation, their commitment will likely enjoy follow-through.

Based on their collaborative work, Board members might begin to see new ways to do ministry, or new ways to continue their ministry that includes the needs of the people next door. If a pastor brings a plan that's based on her personal theological reflection, she may cut off the opportunity for everyone to see what needs to be done and see it together.

Collaboration begins with listening dialogically, but it's more than listening. It's an art of conversation. This section includes the third part of David's story in which he goes to Africa to work with a church in the southern part of the continent. As you read it, note what's new in this situation.

---

### BONGANI'S STORY

Bongani grew up in a rural home in Africa, tending cattle and living in a mud, thatched-roof hut. His family belongs to an indigenous Christian group that emphasizes ritual, disciplined social practices and ecstatic religious experiences. As a young adult he moved to a big city for work. There he met a group of evangelical Christians.

Bongani is now in his late twenties. In the city he works 6 days per week in a factory. His workday begins at 6:00 in the morning and he comes home at 6:00 at night. Bongani is trying to earn enough money to pay the Bride Price so that he can marry and have his own home. In southern Africa it is dark by 7:00 and it is dangerous to go out on the streets after dark. Bongani is a member of David's church. On Sundays, worship services start at 9:00 and last for 2 hours, The rest of the day, Bongani dedicates to restoring himself for work on Monday.

He spends his life in one of several places: in an overcrowded boarding house, at work, at church or occasionally visiting his family. On feast-days and holidays the patterns shifts. Great importance is attached to celebrations because people don't have to work. Big spiritual events are planned on feast-days. As he begins to know his pastor better, Bongani asks David to guide the development of his spiritual life.

## SEEING THE SITUATION

In response to Bongani's request, David looked for ways to enable the African man to carry out the pattern for discipleship that he'd brought with him to Africa. As he talked with Bongani, the African appeared very interested and sincere, but didn't follow-through at any point. David was completely frustrated.

If David considered this opportunity to become collaborative, he couldn't address the lack of connection with Bongani until he found a way to listen to scripture from an African perspective. After observing Bongani's social and cultural context, engaging with material written from an African perspective and turning to scripture through *Lectio Divina*, he was able to gain new insight. Note however, that these conversations are still between David and God and David with himself.

In a sacred reading of scripture, David found that Acts 20:7-12 describes a young man, Eutychus, who listened to the Apostle Paul late into the night. Eutychus was sitting high up on a ledge. He dozed off and died from a fall from his third-storey perch. As David reflected on the compassion Paul showed Eutychus and the whole community by restoring the young man to life, the Holy Spirit nudged him to realize that the cultural world of this young man was much more like Bongani's world than it was like his own Canadian world.

In considering the compassion that moved Paul to raise Eutychus from the dead, David realized that scripture was written for Bongani's world as well as his own—a world where hard working, day-laborers only had time for meetings in the middle of the night and were therefore prone to falling asleep. David was reassured there was a way for discipleship to take place in a context that didn't include the luxury, leisure and the personal privacy of the materialism and individualism that shaped his Canadian, disciplinary practices. Through a process of self-examination, David was able to strip away some cultural assumptions from his view of discipleship so that practices could be found for this new context. As he thought about Jesus' love for every marginalized person he encountered, David also came face-to-face with the racism that had impacted his complete frustration with the African man.

Sensitively reading scripture altered David's feeling toward Bongani's situation. He realized he was steeped in a superior attitude toward his African brother. He came to see that right feeling (orthopathy) undergirds orthodoxy (right thinking) and orthopraxy (right practice). The dissonance engendered by what looked to David like failure to make Bongani into a disciple of Jesus Christ, eventually revealed itself as a desire to make Bongani into a carbon copy of himself. He addressed feelings of frustration and failure by renewing his interest in African culture. He saw aspects of his own worldview in a new way. He wanted to see this new world through Bongani's eyes.[1] This powerful feeling challenged and even altered his expectations for how someone acts out being a follower of Jesus Christ.

But even this new feeling couldn't enable David to find appropriate practices for Bongani's context. He was so unaware of the implications of his own culture he couldn't be helpful if he worked all by himself on the problem. He needed to collaborate in order to find jointly satisfying practices for this new situation. He was so accustomed to working issues out all by himself that he couldn't think outside that large Western cultural framework. He saw scripture from that framework as well.

In order to perceive the individualism David brought to his practice of discipleship, it's important to notice an educational bias in western education that limits potential to learn how to reflect theologically, if Bongani's situation is taken into account. Recall differences between Vygotsky and Piaget referred to earlier. David's understanding of how people learn is based on Piaget's perspectives; that is, what people achieve in learning, they do so all on their own. Perhaps a way forward for David will include a careful analysis of his own assumptions about achievement and a new effort to engage with African understandings of how people learn and what achievement might look like for them. Vygotsky's approach, based as it was on Russian culture, may provide a better lens for David to look through as he tries to understand the situation he and Bongani can now find a way to face together.

---

### EXERCISE: COLLABORATIVE THEOLOGICAL DISCUSSION

Suppose David is part of a group that works together theologically to try to understand how to be effective in the Southern African situation. If you were leading that group, and intended to be collaborative, you might follow a process such as the one outlined below:

**Step #1: Establish the Situation**

Clarifying Questions:

- Is there anything you don't understand about Bongani's situation?

- List your questions on a flip chart.

- Where might you find the information to these questions?

- How might that new information impact how you see this situation?

- How would you describe/depict the situation that David finds himself in?

- How would you describe/depict the situation that Bongani finds himself in?

Artful and Active Listening Questions:

- Has anyone in the group had a similar situation?

- What makes your experience similar and what makes it different?

- What are the core elements of your experience?

- What happened in that situation, to you or to other people?

- What were some of your thoughts and feelings?

- Were there universal needs that you can identify in your situation?

- What are global themes to identify in your situation?

- What does Bongani's personal life story tell us?

- Name some of his universal needs.

- What seems unique to his situation?

- What are some of the generative themes in this situation?

- How might we summarize what we've been hearing?

- Does anyone have insights on ways forward in this situation?

- How might we check out these insights to see if they're reasonable?

Listening to Scripture:

- What is the essence of discipleship?

- What do we need to pass on about discipleship?

- What do people need to have to grow up in the fullness of God?

- What do you know about the essentials of following Jesus?

- What biblical verses, stories or images come to mind that relate to the situation?

- What more do you need to know?

### TALKING TOGETHER

Dialogical conversation enables those involved to think about situations that are typified by dissonance. In dialogue, talking is a precursor to thinking. A human capacity to learn to think during dialogical conversation develops in childhood, as mentioned. How then do we learn to reflect theologically through engaging in dialogical conversation? At the start, we can notice the situation we find ourselves in and find ways to be collaborative. While it's true that learning to talk and think based on talking begins in childhood, it's never too late to learn how to be dialogical, especially if we find opportunities to be with people who already know how to do it and who are willing to come along side us to provide the proximal zone of development Vygotsky thought created the best learning environments.

What are some of the skills of conversing and where do people learn them? We often find ourselves conversing with others who have very different perspectives on a situation. In the following scenario, a family gathered to celebrate an important event. As they began to converse around the dinner table, the dissonant emotion that erupted surprised everyone. The following comments capture the dissonance in an otherwise congenial dinner party.

> The people in this conversation sincerely wanted to apply their Christian faith to ordinary life, but….
>
> [Michael] "This war we're hearing about on the news is a travesty! How can any so-called Christian President justify such destruction in the name of 'fighting terrorism'?"
>
> [Joan] Well, I think he's a very sincere man and he's doing the best job he can. The Christian radio program I listen to told the story of how he became a Christian. The person who told the story was the one who led him into a personal relationship with Jesus.
>
> [Michael] "Oh come on, Joan, you can't believe that Christian drivel, that's a marketing program, not information you can use to build your life on."
>
> "Hold on, I happen to agree with Joan," inserted Frank, "the Bible tells us we should respect our leaders and that sometimes they need to use the sword to achieve peace for the greater good. Wasn't it Augustine, or Calvin, who said some wars can be justified?"
>
> [Melissa] "Yeah but the Bible also says we should love justice, show mercy and walk humbly with God. Those values don't seem to surface in the war rhetoric I hear."
>
> [Michael] "And people like Saddam Hussein, aren't they the most innocent people of all, right?"

### LISTENING TO SCRIPTURE

This conversation is an example of talking together in which Christians seek to make sense of the world in light of their faith.

It's an intersection of worldviews, assumptions and values that emerge from their own personal worldviews.

If collaborative theological reflection is conjoint educational activity, how does it become successful? Christianity requires a blended combination of obedience and reason. Several well-known issues in the New Testament pressured the early Church to talk with each other about complex and difficult issues that were even more explosive than the table talk that erupted in dissonance in the scenario described above.

As one example, in Acts 6:1-7 there was conflict due to the Greek widow's claim that they weren't being treated fairly. In addition, the early Church had to decide about eating meat offered to idols. And they had to clarify sexual morality. There was always the white noise of idolatry. And not the least, there was the issue of circumcision. Early believers had to agree on essential rules of the faith. How did they blend obedience and reason? How did they hear the Holy Spirit above the din of culture and the hue and cry of legalism?

In Acts 15 we have a sketch of a collective inquiry that set a precedent for communal dialogue around issues of ultimate concern. Many Jewish Christians held the view that circumcision was a symbol of loyalty to God and membership within the faith community. This view may have been appropriate in Jewish Jerusalem, but it didn't play well in Gentile Antioch. The text indicates that a sharp dispute erupted when some well-meaning believers attempted to introduce the teaching about circumcision to the believers in Antioch.

Paul and Barnabas had recently returned from intercultural ministry in southern Turkey, and were asked to address this theological dissonance with the Jerusalem elders. The text suggests that in the gathering of elders a process of collective reflection ensued. A variety of leaders expressed their viewpoints, citing various case studies and personal experiences. It appears that James served as a facilitator of the discussion and ultimately summarized their reflections. The written report of findings includes reference to the active presence of the Holy Spirit in their reflection process.

It appears that the Jerusalem elders learned to reflect theologically and collaboratively. They accepted the centrality of Jesus' words. They knew the Holy Spirit could be trusted to guide them in the right way. They sought God's character, holiness, mercy, patience and purity, as their guiding principles for thought and action. The situation boiled with issues that were cultural and religious, personal and communal. Yet they came to a resolve and made a decision. Then, they took action. They wrote a letter to all believers in which they established the rules they thought should be relied upon. They also continued to learn what their decision meant as they went along.

As Christianity spread to cultures that weren't Jewish, early believers had to reframe their expectations for faithfulness by taking the known world into account. We observe a pattern in the New Testament of action and then reflection followed by action and then reflection (and so on) until their ability to reflect theologically increased. But how does collaborative theological reflection work?

Let's gather up a few threads at this point. The focus for theological reflection is a situation that's destabilizing. Conversation begins with a feeling that something doesn't make sense. During theological reflection, people explore the event to see what it teaches about their current assumptions, values and habits. Destabilizing events leave people unsettled and the issue unresolved, so that they create dissonance. Feelings run high. As people try to discover what's going on, they can learn to observe behavior—their own and other people's—and note assumptions and commitments that influence how people see the situation itself. As they consider their observations, and insights arising from them, they can decide whether they want to continue believing and acting in these ways.

The process of Collaborative Theological Reflection is represented in the following model:

## THEOLOGICAL REFLECTION MODEL #4.

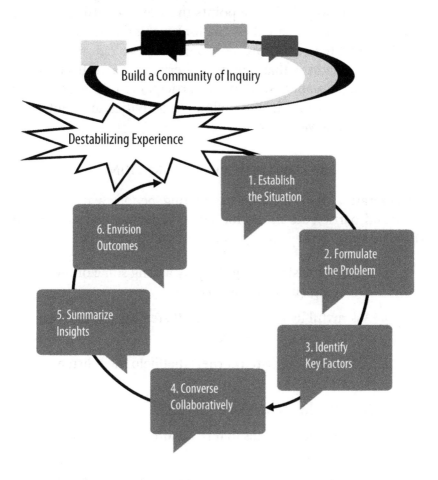

*(Sheffield and Bellous, 2001)*

The Bible needs to inform each dimension of the collaborative process represented in Collaborative Theological Reflection. Yet often we don't know how to bring scripture to bear on our situations. We may be caught up in the interplay of desires, personal and global narratives that fail to understand what the biblical narratives promise. Unless we articulate universal needs, generative themes and global contexts for a destabilizing event, the help offered by scripture is hard to access. The intersection of scripture with life impacts the generative themes that, in turn, further our conversation and push us along our ongoing journey of transformation. Scripture points the way forward, out of the blind spots that populate the situations we find ourselves in.

To bring life to scripture, collaborative theological reflection is a conversation that invites everyone to reflect on a destabilizing situation so that all participants in the group are in some way involved. The following activities are central to collaboration in Model #4.

### ELEMENTS OF COLLABORATION

Collaborative discussion occurs among people who sit at the table and participate in the following activities. They **establish the situation,** as they engage in the following activities:

- Hear the destabilizing story by asking some of the clarifying questions listed earlier
- Ask artful listening questions (listed earlier) that focus on their own experiences
- Ask questions (listed earlier) that help them listen to scripture
- Identify the main issues
- Tell personal stories that relate directly to the destabilizing event
- Make suggestions based on personal expectations, stated as such
- Ask questions that arise from personal experience, assumptions and expectations
- Convey an initial collaborative depiction of the situation
- Establish the essential dissonance in the situation
- Identify on a scale of 1-10 how important the dissonance is to them personally

- Probe the dissonance [rather than poking each other with pointy sticks]
- Name the trap that's destabilizing the people involved in the situation
- Inquire of scripture
- Assess cultural influences
- Identify conflicting interests
- Use analogies
- Establish priorities
- Envision a good future given the situation and its issues
- Retell the story to reveal the influence of theological reflection
- Plan action (the person who brought the destabilizing story)
- Take action
- Remain attentive to what's going on as a result of the action taken
- Learn from what happens when the revised story is incorporated into experience
- Use healthy reason

The section that follows is an outline in more detail of the whole process of collaborative theological reflection as it relates to Model #4, i.e., Collaborative Theological Reflection.

**PROCESS FOR COLLABORATIVE THEOLOGICAL REFLECTION**

The following elements help focus collaborative theological conversations so that reflection is held accountable by Christian scripture, orthodox tradition, examined experience, healthy reason, as well as being informed by culture and personal worldviews of those involved in the inquiry. When a group of learners decide to embark upon a collaborative process there are several identifiable steps that can be taken. These steps are as follows:

**Build a Community of Inquiry:** This work needs to be done among a group of colleagues, congregants, or friends. This isn't personal reflection shared in a group. It's group reflection that calls everyone to participate in an environment of mutual respect grounded on models exemplified in Scripture. When the disciples argued among themselves about leadership, Jesus gently redirected them and taught a model of servant leadership. He wanted the quality of character in his disciples to be their love for one another.

When we encounter destabilizing experiences, as we inevitably do, our growth will be most profoundly impacted by being part of a group of Christians who have already learned what it means to be a community of inquiry that's characterized by trust and truth. If we aren't part of such a group, this kind of environment of inquiry needs to be developed before the work of collaborative reflection can happen.

**Establish the Situation and Name the Destabilizing Concern:** Collaborative conversation begins with a destabilizing event, the moment of surprise that no previous knowledge and experience can explain easily. As participants seek to explore a way through dissonance, they make a core commitment. Each participant is willing and able to put an emotionally laden story (destabilizing event) on the table. Sometimes, not everyone can connect to a particular situation. In that case, it's important to acknowledge that lack of connection to the situation at the start, because some around the table aren't yet aware of how their experience is similar to the one that's on the table.

If the group is intentionally building a community of inquiry characterized by truth and trust, stories are placed on the table in a safe environment with a group that's willing to reflect on, and renovate their knowledge of what's going on in the situation. Willingness is a first step. As a group establishes the situation, they use linguistic and non-linguistic forms for communication so that everyone, to everyone's satisfaction, unpacks the situation.

This work is complete when everyone involved agrees that the situation's depiction and description capture all of its important aspects. If there's disagreement, those who disagree, even one person, clearly state their position and the interests they have in how they see the situation, and volunteer to wait until more work is done in the following steps. As the process continues, they may agree with the group or they may have new reasons for disagreeing. In that case, the situation needs to be re-presented. It's essential to go back and make sure this person or these people are onside with the way others are seeing the situation, if this is at all possible, without misusing social power to achieve agreement. It's also essential to use healthy reason as this work is being done.

**Formulate the Problem:** In this third stage the group seeks a common understanding of what happened to produce destabilization. In order for common understanding to emerge individuals need to narrate their experience to the group, answering the basic questions of 'who, what, where, when, and how.' Individuals name aspects of the situation to represent key issues or concerns for them. These wider issues or generative themes arise from the situation and the problem it contains and become the focus of inquiry and learning.

Universal needs and generative themes are listed at this point. As a result, the situation may be seen in a new light. It's important to gather these changes in perspective on it, and include them in how the group understands what's going on. Often at this stage, it becomes apparent that people in the situation are trapped by expectations and assumptions they hold or that have hold of them. Naming the trap and envisioning what it looks and feels like is important as a first step in releasing oneself from that trap.

As an example, David was trapped in his desire to meet Bongani's need and his inability to do so successfully. As a result of reflecting on this aspect of his involvement, and not treating his own worldview dismissively through the use of unhealthy reason, he came to see that his superior attitude was getting in his way and needed to be transformed by Jesus' love. He also recommitted himself to acting out the truth that Jesus loves Bongani and knows his situation, as much as Jesus loves David and knows his background experience.

Once David acknowledged his racism, he could look at the situation with fresh eyes. He could then acknowledge that believing one's own way is best is normal, but that that belief needs to be addressed by God's sovereign love for every one of God's children, regardless of their social location, race, gender or economic situation. David came to see with Peter, as the vision was let down while he was on the rooftop, and before he went to Cornelius's house, that we're not to call anyone unclean that God has called clean. (Acts 10: 9-29]

If anyone had accused David of being racist before he came to this realization, he would have denied it vehemently and felt very insulted. What he learned in this situation is that his worldview itself contained this superiority and that it's simply the way we're all socialized in our cultures of origin. While he couldn't help privileging his own way of doing things at the start, he could now see a new opportunity to take biblical approaches to discipleship and, along with his African brothers and sisters, he could learn with them how best to become disciples of Jesus Christ in this new situation. These insights could emerge for David as he truthfully and trustfully engages with his community of inquiry.

For instance, David could describe to this group his deep concern to find a meaningful discipleship process that could take account of Bongani's situation. In the context of being in a safe environment, he could loosen his grip on his own way of being a disciple in this context. The group could help him reflect on the losses and worries that this move might entail. He might also realize he feels trapped by the expectation/assumption that there is only one right way to be a disciple. With a cohort of interested and supportive people, some of whom are mature African brothers and sisters, he could describe his understanding of the situation and his initial responses to it. The group would then work together to clarify the situation by employing everyone's perspectives on it. Other group members could share similar incidents. Then together, the group would seek to identify and formulate the problem by using collaborative theological reflection.

**Identify Key Factors:** In the fourth stage, the group seeks to identify key factors and the dynamics that seem significant to understanding the problem under reflection. For example, what are key factors in feeling trapped in the way that David does? Individuals in the group contribute their perspectives, which they believe are affecting the destabilizing concern. These may come in the form of assumptions, attitudes, interpersonal dynamics, social forces, cultural issues and practices and power dynamics that are seen by group members as important to the situation.

Key factors lead to further exploration within the collaborative conversation. David needs to understand the significance of, as some examples,

- Diverse learning styles
- Generational factors influencing culture
- Marriage practices and teaching practices in Africa
- The role of different cultural values and lifestyles between Canada and Africa

During collaboration, the group puts all these factors on the table, raising some issues that David wouldn't have imagined, if left on his own.

**Converse Collaboratively:** This is a massive brainstorming exercise. Ideas and thoughts are expressed without being evaluated as they come up; they're merely accepted at face value as potential areas for further conversation. Insights from group members' academic studies, reading, or theoretical knowledge are drawn into the conversation to shed light on the problem. Individuals seek to discern how the dissonance connects with their core values, convictions, and life history. How do wider issues (global narratives) interact with personal narratives? What unknown factors may still exist for full analysis? Where are the blind spots?

**Summarize Insights:** At stage six, the collaborative group needs to summarize their learning in a manner that will aid further development and change. What is the Holy Spirit saying through this process? Are there places where the group is in agreement and disagreement? What has surfaced from the collaborative reflection that affects the way people around the table now think or feel about this situation? Are there diagrams or symbols (non-linguistic representations) that have emerged to explain what's going on? Has a way forward shown up as yet?

**Envision Outcomes**: Finally, new responses are required that give direction to a fresh manner of addressing the area of dissonance. Collectively, the group identifies practical steps forward. What core values or assumptions are needed in order to adjust to or accept the emerging outcomes? How will the group re-imagine the situation and reconstruct plausible actions or changes in thinking and practice of people involved in the situation?

**Theological Reflection Model #4** outlines the main elements of the process of collaborative theological reflection. Examine the diagram and apply the process to a destabilizing situation that you're facing or that someone else has brought to you. In order to carry out the process, you need to engage with a group of people who can commit to engaging with one another in building a community of inquiry that will eventually be characterized by trust and truthfulness. You might invite a Sunday school class or a Bible study group into the process with you. If you are a seminary student, you may have opportunities to work collaboratively during your course work.

---

**Exercise: Collaborative Reflection**

Using the passage from Acts 15:1-14, which is an account of an Early Church controversy, go through the steps of Collaborative Theological Inquiry with a group of people who've committed to working towards building a community of inquiry.

---

### CONCLUSION

Collaborative theological reflection can look like a lot of work—and, it is. Yet, if a collaborative process takes place and is maintained as an ongoing way of addressing destabilizing events, David and Bongani will learn from scripture how to be worthy disciples of Jesus Christ. Something new emerges in their relationship and in the church. When the work of a community of inquiry arrives at new insights, the overall ministry they engage in is deeply impacted. As an example from David's case study, collaborative theological conversation allows for equality before God that was so characteristic of the Early Church and is implicit in Jesus' words and practice.

How might collaborative inquiry provide for the changes in the ministries that Jake and Marjorie lead? How would talking together with other believers, if these believers don't judge but understand the call of Christ on their own lives, heal the generative theme of isolation?

Are there issues in your personal life and ministry you long to learn more about, or change?

The evidence that collaboration has taken place is that all participants see a presenting problem in a new way and alter their theological understanding of it in an environment of trust and truth telling. The outcome of a community of inquiry approach allows new insights to become apparent or new reasons for position previously held to be seen for their role in how believers think and act. While people may not completely agree as they work collaboratively, they can work together.

The impetus for theological reflection isn't to make people change, although meaningful change is more likely to occur as understanding and relationships mature. Rather, it's to speak the truth in love in the company of other believers who listen artfully and actively. The point of theological reflection is to become more mature by learning more about God. Learning more about God comes about by setting the way we see the world alongside scriptures that convey what God is like, as opposed to how we imagine God to be, when it's simply based on our own personal histories.

Committed Christian belief has the effects of producing maturity in the human heart. Faith maturity is missing in many of our churches in North America. Church leaders want worship services to be sanctuaries where the Messiah finds lost people. The time is ripe for renewal. Christian faith isn't just profoundly true; it's also beautiful because it fits our humanity and all of its needs and foibles.

Christians who are strongly committed to collaborative theological reflection come to experience talking together as an approach that eventually becomes dialogical. May this book allow its readers to engage in a rewarding and revitalizing practice that's capable of rejuvenating Christian community and transforming our lives to be like Jesus' own life. In that renewal, we can refresh our commitment to the Great Commission that was handed down to us by our Lord Jesus Christ. He summoned us to go into all the world and make disciples, baptizing them in the name of Father, Son and Holy Spirit and teaching them everything that the Living Lord Jesus still commands us to know, to be and to do.

# Notes

1. Dan Sheffield, *The Multicultural Leader: Developing a catholic personality,* Second Edition, (Toronto: Clements Publishing, 2015), 91.

# APPENDIX

Evan came to a small town church right out of Seminary. He had wanted to be a pastor as long as he could remember and was grateful that his wife Susan supported his ministry. She got a job in a small town nearby as a grade one teacher. Since Evan felt comfortable in small town culture, he was readily accepted by everyone he met. All the townsfolk knew who he was. He liked the feeling of being known by everyone because he thought it offered opportunity to minister to anyone.

Evan was also committed to increasing the church, in particular by reaching out to folks who had Grown up on the "wrong side of town." His parents had ministered to the poor all his life and he deeply respected them for it. He wanted the church to be a place where everyone was welcome and where the gospel was both preached about and lived out.

He soon saw how the church was organized and thought he understood how decisions got made. Clearly the Wilson and Whiteside families were key leaders in the church. Members of both families were on two primary church boards: the Deacons' Board and the Board of Management.

Early in January of his first year, he brought to the Deacons' Board an idea for ministering among the disadvantaged citizens of the town. To begin, he would lead them in theologically reflecting on poverty and its causes. Before the meeting, George Whiteside, the chair of Deacons, saw his proposal drawn out on a paper that he had copied for all the Board members. That night, George chaired the session so slowly there was no time left to introduce John's idea.

When Evan approached George after the meeting to ask why they hadn't addressed his agenda item, George waved his hand in Evan's direction and said: "We don't do that sort of thing here" and left the room. Evan was speechless and stood alone in the room for a long time wondering what went wrong.

Sophie has been with the congregation for five years and wants to leave. She sees a pattern she can no longer endure. For example, the other night at the Deacons' Meeting the same discussion came up for what she was sure was the tenth time.

As pastor, she introduced the idea of ministering in a Seniors' Complex a few blocks from the church. When she first mentioned it, everyone said it was a great idea. After that meeting, Sophie negotiated with the Complex, promising that the church would bring a service of worship to the residents, once per month. That was two years ago. As part of the service, she visits with people and prays with them individually. The seniors like to sing hymns, so she plays the piano, leads worship and also preaches. She is committed to the ministry but cannot get others to help her.

She knows the ministry is very much appreciated by the residents. Her own mother is in the Complex. She is overwhelmed and angry because people who share her view that it is important won't come to minister to people that so obviously appreciate having the service. She thought about the seniors and decided to try again.

She raised the subject at the meeting by telling stories of how the residents appreciate having her come. The Deacons expressed real interest in the ministry and said they thought it was a good idea and important for the church to be involved. Sophie told them more stories to outline some of the residents' spiritual needs. In the visioning part of the meeting she brought out earlier visioning exercises in which they had together outlined some of the ways they could minister to these seniors. They had made lists of what could be done and she went over these lists and they brainstormed new items to add to them. People agreed that they could probably do some of these tasks. They expressed the importance of doing ministry to seniors. When she asked who could come the next Thursday, everyone grew silent.

After the meeting she spoke to the Chair, Charles, and asked him what he might do to make sure people followed through. She was tired of having to ask people repeatedly. It made her feel like a nag and she abhorred that feeling. She told him she hoped the Deacons would be so moved by her stories that they would agree to come on Thursday mornings. Many of them were available because they were either at home or retired. Some of them could take time off when they chose and could certainly make time in their schedules to come once a month. Sophie expressed frustration to Charles that people would talk about ministry but not do it.

Charles went home and his wife Joan asked about the meeting. She had been a Deacon as well when Sophie first came. Joan laughed when he told her they were brainstorming about ministry at the Seniors' Complex. She recalled numerous discussions about the very same topic when she was a Deacon. "I can't believe that you are still talking about ministering to the seniors and no one is actually doing it. " Joan's frustration with this very sort of problem was the reason she left the Deacons' Board and she vowed she would never come back. The next morning she phoned Sophie to commiserate with her and volunteered to pray about the issue. Sophie agreed to get together for prayer, but she wondered what issue Joan was referring to and felt hesitant about the meeting.

## FRED'S STORY

Fred had been in ministry for ten years as the pastor of a medium-sized rural congregation. He then went to a large urban church as Associate Pastor. He is responsible for pastoral care, small groups, youth and outreach. As part of his |ob, he works closely with the senior pastor, Jeremy, but has noticed what he thinks are serious problems because the former pastor, Sam, is retired yet still attends the church. Many members continue to refer to Sam as their pastor, and go to him for pastoral counseling,.

The church has a long history of very good preaching. Apparently Sam was an excellent preacher and put a lot of time into pastoral visitation, which were his only other responsibilities as senior pastor. He shared the visitation responsibility with a full-time pastoral counsellor. As a result, the church was accustomed to being visited regularly and often.

Fred feels rushed and busy most of the time. He preaches once per month, in the evening, so has little contact with members in the role of preacher. He also spends time with Jeremy who is at his wits end with what he calls interference from Sam. Jeremy told Fred that whenever he brings an idea to a congregational meeting he expects close friends of Sam's to argue against his idea, no matter what it is. Fred likes Jeremy and enjoys going for coffee whenever they can. Jeremy is 10 years older than Fred and was also pastor in a medium-sized rural church at the start of his ministry.

In addition to the other complexities, Fred has no success working, with the Children's Pastor, Lois. Whenever he tries to coordinate a meeting to discuss plans that involve church families, she is late for the meeting or doesn't show up. He has decided that she resents his leadership. She has been at the church for I 5 years in her present role. Her position is part-time, but she spends many more than 20 hours per week at the church.

Fred feels that communication is a serious problem in the community. Events are planned but members don't show up. He is beginning to feel he made a big mistake coming to this church. Did he hear a call here, or not?

Fred decided to have a meeting with Jeremy and Lois. He asked Jeremy to lead the meeting but Jeremy declined. Fred wasn't prepared for the angry silence when they did meet. As usual, Lois was late. So for the most part, it turned out to be another conversation with Jeremy. When Lois did come, Jeremy said very little and Lois said less. When he went home, Fred felt frustrated and expressed it to his wife by saying, " How can we have a meeting about communication if no one will talk?" As he processed the meeting, with his wife, she asked why Jeremy refused to lead it. Fred said he didn't know. The only time during the meeting the two men talked freely was while they complained about Sam. During that part of the meeting, Lois was particularly quiet. Fred was afraid she would tell Sam what they had said about him. He told his wife he felt tired of it all.

## JUDY'S STORY

Judy is in her early forties. She and her husband have no children. He is an executive, making a very good salary so she decided to leave a teaching position she held for twelve years and work for a Mission Agency. In her job, she developed administrative skill and worked for five years as Vice-President of the company. At this point, she has been with the Mission Agency for eight years. She coordinates relationships between churches and missionaries so that local communities partner with churches around the world. She is very successful. The project has grown and is flourishing. Her work comes under the general Administrator of the Agency. She has no decision-making power with respect to her program.

Recently, the Director of the Agency offered her a position with increased responsibility and higher salary in the area of Funding and Recruitment. Judy considered the opportunity and prayed about it but felt no inclination to change jobs. She felt called to the program and that sense of calling had not changed. She turned down the opportunity to shift her role.

But as a result of her reflection, she decided to approach the Director for a raise. In her eight years at the Agency, she had no increase in salary, although others had. When she came to the Agency she gave up a good salary but told herself that sacrifice was part of her calling. After all, she didn't need it. The program she administered had increased and now she had four times the number of people working under her than when she came. If they were willing to offer her more salary for the position she rejected, surely they would give her a raise, she thought. The success of the program was clear so she gathered documentation concerning her program and asked for an appointment with the general Administrator. At the meeting she presented her case for a raise. The Administrator got very angry. At one point, she handed him her documents and he took them and threw them down on his desk. He raised his arms and yelled, accusing her of greed. He was furious with the documentation and shouted at her, challenging her as to why she could have been as deceitful and so sneaky that she would compile information behind his back.

Judy was stunned. After the Administrator stopped yelling, before he said anything else, she got out of her chair and left the office. She managed to keep from crying until she got back to her own desk and closed the door behind her.

# INDEX

focusing, 32, 35-43, 55, 59, 63,
66-68, 77-79

G

generative theme, 85-89, 91, 92,
96-99, 138, 151, 152, 160,
166, 209, 213, 217, 220

global narrative, 213, 219

God concept, 43, 108-110, 114,
117, 121, 142, 162

H

healthy reason, 31, 32, 34,
36-38, 43, 44, 48, 52, 53, 55,
70, 71, 75, 80, 99, 141, 142,
215, 217

I

inexperienced monk, 71-73, 77,
86

inform, ix, 3, 25, 48, 51, 67, 88,
93, 99, 107, 114, 116, 139,
144, 166, 189, 213, 215

L

leaving home, 59, 60, 173

lectio divina, ix, x, 24-26, 28, 43,
100, 101, 108, 140-143, 150,
151, 155, 156, 194, 206

N

narrative inquiry, 114

nous, 45, 46, 48, 49, 51, 53, 54,
56, 71

P

personal inquiry, 19, 22, 85, 100,
159

personal narrative, ix, 88, 93, 98,
119, 166, 219

personality, 67, 134-136, 138,
139, 177

R

representation of meaning, 201

returning home, 55, 59, 71, 173

S

sapientia, 53, 54, 101, 140, 141,
143, 145, 147, 156

self-observation, 23, 33, 34, 43,
44, 49, 66-71, 76-78, 140,
141, 156

soulful thinking, 53, 100, 156,
182

speaking the truth in love, 35,
42, 60, 99

spiritual healing, 66, 68

spiritual needs, 105, 125-127,
142, 151, 224

spirituality, 32, 33, 72, 103-106,
132-137, 140, 161

T

theological reflection, ix, x, 3, 4,
6-14, 16-23, 31-35, 42-46,
48, 49, 51, 53-55, 59, 60,
62-65, 67-70, 76, 78-80, 85,
88, 90, 91, 97, 99-102, 105,
107-109, 113-119, 125, 126,
129, 130, 134, 139, 140, 142,
145, 151, 152, 155-161,
165-167, 169-171, 174,
177-180, 183, 185, 186, 189,
190, 193-194, 201, 203, 205,
211-215, 219-221

transform, 67, 105, 114, 180

transmit, 104, 106, 166

U

unhealthy reason, 32, 34, 36-38,
43, 44, 64, 65, 67, 69-71, 75,
78, 90, 141, 146, 150, 171,
217

CPSIA information can be obtained
at www.ICGtesting.com
Printed in the USA
LVHW042113201222
735632LV00004B/461